THE
RAILWAY
ENTHUSIASTS
ALMANAC

Peter Kelly

Eric Dobby Publishing

Published by Eric Dobby Publishing Ltd,
12 Warnford Road, Orpington, Kent BR6 6LW

A catalogue record for this book is available from the
British Library

ISBN 1-85882-008-1

Typeset in 9pt on 10pt Plantin by
Blackpool Typesetting Services Ltd, Blackpool.

Printed and bound in Great Britain by
BPCC Hazell Books Ltd
Member of BPCC Ltd

Introduction

RAILWAYS have played a vital role in the development of the world as we know it, but it might be tempting, at the beginning of any post-industrial era, to view them merely as an important historical subject. In view of today's concerns about the environment however, no one can doubt that railways will be required to play an increasingly important role in the future.

Preparing a truly pocket-sized reference book on such a huge subject can only be an act of compromise, for in less than two centuries man's knowledge has grown from the application of steam to lumbering contraptions only just able to move under their own power, to the use of electricity to hurtle sleek supertrains along at well over 200 mph.

Although Great Britain, as the cradle of the Industrial Revolution, was at the forefront of railway development, the 'iron road' quickly spread to weave its glistening web across whole continents, and the achievements of each and every country involved merit a book many times the size of this one!

The Railway Almanac confines its pages exclusively to Britain, briefly examining a variety of the locomotives – workaday, outstanding and even experimental – which have played their part in our railway history. Nearly 120 types are featured, taking in steam, diesel, electric and even gas turbine. The list could just as easily have been 500! I hope you have as much pleasure reading about them as I did in doing the research!

The world's first *public* railway utilising steam power (although by no means exclusively, because at first, passengers tended to be hauled by horses) was undoubtedly the Stockton & Darlington Railway,

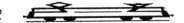

which opened in 1825, but the idea of railways, waggon-ways or plate-ways providing confining tracks for the movement of heavy loads – and even the use of primitive steam engines on such tracks – goes back still further. As the story has been told many times before, and in far more detail than could be contemplated here, such trail-blazers have been excluded from the general content of this book, although they certainly merit a mention in this introduction.

When Cornish engineer Richard Trevithick won a 500-guinea wager in 1804 by proving that his geared locomotive could move a load of ten tons of iron and numerous 'passengers' some nine miles between Pen-y-Daren (there are numerous spellings!) and the canal at Abercynon, South Wales, the idea of steam traction was just a novelty, and although he demonstrated 'Catch-Me-Who-Can' on a circular track in London like some extravagant fairground ride, he was to die a poor man.

Steam was soon put to use on colliery railways, however, and pioneering types included the locomotives of Matthew Murray and John Blenkinsop introduced in 1812 for the Middleton Colliery Railway, Leeds, Christopher Blackett and John Hedley's 1813 'Puffing Billy' built for the Wylam Colliery Railway, and George Stephenson's 'Locomotion' of 1825 which worked on the Stockton & Darlington Railway.

It was the Liverpool & Manchester Railway, opened five years later in 1830, and relying on steam power for the transport of both goods and passengers, from which the railways we know today really developed. In 1829, in anticipation of that railway's opening, important locomotive trials were organised at Rainhill, Lancashire. The three major runners were George and son Robert Stephenson's 'Rocket', Timothy Hackworth's 'Sans Pareil' and John Ericsson's 'Novelty'.

In the event 'Rocket' was the clear winner. It had two inclined outside cylinders driving rather unstably from high up at the rear rather than low down at the front of the locomotive, a multi-tube

boiler, a primitive blastpipe and a water-jacket firebox, setting the stage for many features that were to be further developed and refined in generations of steam locomotives to come. 'Sans Pareil', much heavier and more sure-footed with its coupled driving wheels, was almost certainly the strongest, and perhaps in these two entries could be seen the early evolution of locomotives into passenger and freight types. The lightweight 'Novelty' unfortunately broke down, although it was almost certainly the fastest of the three. It would have lost out on haulage capacity, though.

When the 'Rocket 150' celebrations re-enacted the Rainhill Trials along virtually the same stretch of track in 1980, working replicas of each of the original entrants took part in the parade. There is also a working replica of 'Locomotion' at the Beamish Museum in County Durham, and of one of Trevithick's locomotive at the Ironbridge Gorge Museum. Both 'Puffing Billy' and what remains of the much modified original 'Rocket' are at London's Science Museum.

In the ensuing decades, steam locomotives developed rapidly, the largest of them to be found on the 7ft gauge (it was actually 7ft¼in!) of Isambard Kingdom Brunel's Great Western Railway. This undoubtedly allowed plenty of space for comfort, not to mention train stability, but when 'railway mania' swept the country so that virtually every town and village had its own station, a 'standard gauge' of 4ft 8 ½in (it was actually 4ft 8⅜ in!) was adopted in the interests of uniformity.

Once the basic components of a successful steam engine had been proved in service, design improvements and the consequent increases in speed and haulage capacity quickly followed. By the time rivalry between the East Coast and West Coast routes from London to Scotland had reached a peak in the 1895 'Race to the North', the London & North Western Railway's No. 790 'Hardwicke' – which still survives at the National Railway Museum – was *averaging* 67 mph between Crewe and Carlisle.

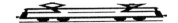

   As the weight of trains steadily grew, so did the
size and power of locomotives, and by 1903 the
Great Western Railway's No. 3440 'City of Truro'
was reputed to have exceeded 100 mph near
Wellington, Somerset, with an 'Ocean Mails'
special. This historic locomotive has also been
preserved and occasionally still sees action today.
By the 1930s, streamlined trains such as the 'Silver
Jubilee' and 'Coronation' of the London & North
Eastern Railway and 'Coronation Scot' of the
London Midland & Scottish Railway were
demonstrating their 100 mph-plus potential in a
series of high-speed runs which culminated in Sir
Nigel Gresley's 'A4' 'Pacific' No. 4468 'Mallard'
breaking the world record for steam in the summer
of 1938 at over 126 mph. This was a far-from-
normal downhill run, however, and resulted in a
broken middle big end bearing. Far more typical
was the 112 mph attained by the first 'A4', No. 2509
'Silver Link' on a trial 'Silver Jubilee' run in the
autumn of 1935 (and coincidentally the same speed
reached by sister locomotive No. 60007 'Sir Nigel
Gresley' when hauling a Stephenson Locomotive
Society special train in 1959), and the 114 mph
reached by LMS 'Princess Coronation' streamliner
No. 6200 'Coronation' in 1937.
   These streamliners though, marked the zenith of
British steam. The Second World War, like the
First before it, had put a terrible strain on Britain's
railway resources, which ended up broken, worn out
and exhausted, and the new emphasis was on
simplicity, reliability and ease of maintenance.
Nationalisation of the Big Four railway companies –
the LNER, LMS, Great Western and Southern –
took effect from 1 January 1948, and although a
useful range of 'standard' steam classes was
introduced from 1951 onwards, the writing was on
the wall for steam.
   Even before nationalisation, work had begun on
diesel electric, straight electric and gas turbine
ideas, and main line diesel electric pioneer No.
10000, built at Derby, even managed to emerge in
1947 with 'LMS' proudly displayed along its body

side. The LMS had introduced a substantial number of diesel shunters too, one type of which formed the basis for a numerous British Railways class. The LNER at Doncaster had already built the first electric locomotive for the Manchester-Sheffield Woodhead route, and had experience of electric traction around Newcastle-upon-Tyne. The Great Western had introduced diesel railcars successfully to some of its services before the war and was looking at gas turbines for main line work, and the Southern, already substantially electrified around London, was designing advanced steam locomotives, electric locomotives and diesel electrics before nationalisation.

The 1955 Modernisation Plan for British Railways put the emphasis on the efficiency and economy of diesel and electric traction, and the widespread pruning of Britain's railway system in the wake of the Beeching Report changed the face of our railways for ever.

Abroad, steam reached its pinnacle in the massive 1941 'Big Boy' 4-8-8-4 locomotives of the Union Pacific Railroad. These giants weighed over 500 tons apiece, had an adhesive weight (ie over the driving wheels) of nearly 250 tons, and could move loads of 6,000 tons up the notorious gradient to Sherman Hill. In the oil-rich United States, however, diesel traction began taking over on several railroads in the 1930s, the Chicago, Burlington & Quincy Railroad's three-car, high-speed diesel electric 'Pioneer Zephyr' averaging 78 mph over the 1,015 miles between Denver and Chicago, and amazingly modern-looking locomotives such as General Motors' Electro-Motive Division's 'E' series A1A-A1A diesel electrics appearing in 1937. The Pennsylvania Railroad's legendary GG1 2 Co-Co 2 electrics, introduced in 1934, remained in service until only a few years ago.

Today, with more modern forms of motive power and – equally importantly – huge advances in the quality of track and signalling making possible average train times that were previously undreamed of (witness the record-breaking run between

London King's Cross and Edinburgh on 26 September 1991 at an average of 112.9 mph, with several peaks at 140 mph), the future of railways is looking brighter than ever.

The Channel Tunnel will link Britain to the high-speed railway systems of mainland Europe, while at home there will be a wholesale blossoming of light rail systems in our city centres. Those at Newcastle, Manchester and Sheffield will be just the start.

Rarely has the future of railways looked more secure.

Wheel arrangements

Not surprisingly, terms such as 'Mogul' and '1 Co-Co 1' which are used when describing the wheel arrangements of steam and modern traction locomotives do not make a great deal of sense to those with a passing rather than all-consuming interest in railways, so I have put together this general guide, and hope it proves useful to many readers.

Steam engines may have:
- driving wheels only
- front carrying wheels and driving wheels
- driving wheels and rear carrying wheels
- front carrying wheels, driving wheels and rear carrying wheels
- separate sets of driving and carrying wheels, as in the case of Beyer-Garratt and Mallet types.

If a locomotive has no front carrying wheels, four driving wheels and no rear carrying wheels, it is described as an 0-4-0. If it carries its water in locomotive-mounted tanks instead of a separate tender, it is described as an 0-4-0T. If it has a curved saddle tank going over the top of the boiler, it is described as an 0-4-0ST, and if it has the high-mounted pannier tanks commonly seen on the Great Western Railway, it is described as an 0-4-0PT. If there are six driving wheels, but no carrying wheels either at the front or rear of the locomotive, it will be an 0-6-0, if there are eight driving wheels an 0-8-0, and so on.

Should the locomotive have no front carrying wheels, two driving wheels and two rear carrying wheels, it would be an 0-2-2. Four front carrying wheels, six driving wheels and two rear carrying wheels would make it a 4-6-2, a type commonly known as 'Pacific'. Similar nicknames have been given to other wheel arrangement types, and these are included in the accompanying list.

O∘	0-2-2	OOOO∘	0-8-2	
∘O∘O∘	4-2-2	∘OOOO	2-8-0	
OO	0-4-0		'Consolid-	
OO∘	0-4-2		ation'	
∘OO	2-4-0	∘OOOO∘	2-8-2	
∘OO∘	2-4-2		'Mikado'	
OO∘∘	0-4-4	∘OOOO∘∘	2-8-4	
∘∘OO	4-4-0	∘∘OOOO∘	4-8-2	
∘∘OO∘	4-4-2	∘∘OOOO∘∘	4-8-4	
	'Atlantic'		'Northern'	
OOO	0-6-0	OOOOO	0-10-0	
OOO∘	0-6-2		'Decapod'	
∘OOO	2-6-0	OOOOO∘	0-10-2	
	'Mogul'	∘OOOOO	2-10-0	
∘OOO∘	2-6-2	∘OO OO∘	2-4-4-2	
	'Prairie'		'Garratt'	
OOO∘∘	0-6-4	∘OOO OOO∘	2-6-6-2	
∘∘OOO	4-6-0		'Garratt'	
∘∘OOO∘	4-6-2	∘OOOO OOOO∘	2-8-8-2	
	'Pacific'	∘∘OOOO OOOO∘∘	4-8-8-4	
OOOO	0-8-0			

An entirely different code is used to describe the wheel arrangements of diesel, electric and gas turbine locomotives, by which *axles* rather than wheels are counted. Numerical figures are used to describe the number of non-powered carrying axles, and letters are used to describe the number of powered axles.

In the case of a diesel electric locomotive with no carrying wheels, but a powered four-wheel bogie at each end utilising a separate traction motor for each axle, this would be known as a Bo-Bo. The 'B' means two axles, and the small 'o' means that each axle is *separately* powered.

If the locomotive were a diesel hydraulic, with each hydraulic transmission being *shared* between the axles of each bogie, the small 'o' would be dropped and it would be described as a B-B.

A locomotive – whether diesel, electric or gas turbine – with a six-wheel bogie at each end, each axle being individually powered, would be a Co-Co. If the locomotive were a 'Western' diesel hydraulic, though, and each hydraulic transmission was shared between three axles, it would be a C-C.

Where carrying wheels are used, as in the case of the late lamented English Electric Type '4s' and 'Peak' diesel electrics (both described in this book), then *numbers* come into it. These classes each had an outer carrying axle at the ends of their six-wheel bogies so were classified 1 Co-Co 1.

Sometimes, as in the case of the class '31' diesel electrics, only the outer two axles of each six-wheel bogie are powered, so the unpowered carrying wheels are in the middle. That makes them A1A-A1A locomotives.

Where outside coupling rods are used, as in the case of the class '08' diesel-electric shunting locomotives, the description reverts to the normal steam one of 0-6-0.

A sample list of modern traction wheel arrangements is given thus:

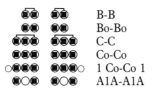

🚃🚃	🚃🚃	B-B
🚃🚃	🚃🚃	Bo-Bo
🚃🚃🚃	🚃🚃🚃	C-C
🚃🚃🚃	🚃🚃🚃	Co-Co
○🚃🚃🚃	🚃🚃🚃○	1 Co-Co 1
🚃○🚃	🚃○🚃	A1A-A1A

Peter Kelly
1 July 1993

Stirling 'Single'

The splendour of Stirling 'Single' No. 1.
Chris Milner

Railway of origin Great Northern
Introduced 1870
Designer Patrick Stirling
Purpose Express passenger
Wheel arrangement 4-2-2
Driving wheel diameter 8ft 1in
Cylinders Two (outside) 18in x 28in
Tractive effort 2,050 lb
Number built 53

Victorian elegance oozed from the beautiful bogie
'Singles' built for express passenger work on the
Great Northern main line by Patrick Stirling, the
GNR's Locomotive Superintendent from 1866 until
1895. Although lightish loads of 190 tons or so were
the norm at that time, the massive 8ft 1in diameter
driving wheels gave the 'Singles' a speed potential
approaching 80 mph, and these 'greyhounds' ruled
the roost until the growing size and weight of trains
made them redundant. They were replaced by the
more powerful 4-4-2 'Atlantic' designs until they,
too, were superseded by the yet more powerful 4-6-2
'Pacifics' which held sway until the end of steam in
Britain. Fortunately, Stirling 'Single' No. 1 is
retained in the National Collection and was steamed
regularly until relatively recently.

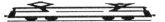

'Terrier' Tank

No. 32670 at Newhaven Shed on 7 June 1962.
R.C. Riley

Railway of origin London, Brighton & South Coast
Railway
Introduced 1872
Designer W. Stroudley
Purpose Light passenger
Wheel arrangement 0-6-0T
Driving wheel diameter 4 ft 0 in
Cylinders Two (inside) 12 in x 20 in
Tractive effort 7,650 lb
Number built 50

Built from 1872 until 1880, the 'Terrier' tank
engines of the LBSCR first worked on London local
trains. Shortly after the turn of the century,
however, some moved to other railways such as the
Isle of Wight and Kent & East Sussex. When
Britain's railways were grouped into four large
operators in 1923, some of these locos were brought
under Southern Railway control, and later passed to
British Railways. Of the ten which, remarkably, still
survive, one of the most interesting is No. 3
'Bodiam'. Originally the LBSCR's No. 70 'Poplar',
it was sold to the K&ESR and became No. 3
'Bodiam'. Years later, it lost its name to become BR
No. 32670, and in this guise notched up ninety
years' service. Today, it is back at the *preserved*
K&ESR with its old identity again.

Adams Radial Tank

Adams Radial No. 488, along with former South Eastern & Chatham Railway 'H' class 0-4-4T No. 263 at Sheffield Park, Bluebell Railway, in May 1982.
Chris Milner

Railway of origin London & South Western Railway
Introduced 1882
Designer W. Adams
Purpose Light Passenger
Wheel arrangement 4-4-2T
Driving wheel diameter 5ft 7in
Cylinders Two (outside) $17\frac{1}{2}$ in x 24 in
Tractive effort 14,920 lb
Number built 71

By a quirk of history, a solitary example of the Adams 4-4-2 radial tank engines, No. 488 (BR No. 30583) survives at the Bluebell Railway, where occasionally it can still be seen in steam. Although seventy-one of these long-wheelbase locomotives were built by a variety of constructors, including Beyer Peacock & Co., Robert Stephenson & Co, and Neilson's from 1882, many had been withdrawn by the time the First World War ended. By 1923, the Southern Railway had only two, used on the sharply curving Lyme Regis branch, but a third was brought back from the East Kent Railway in 1946. The locomotives were so perfectly suited to their particular branch working that they survived into British Railways days, numbered 30582-4, and soldiered on until the very end.

'J15' 0-6-0

The sole surviving 'J15' 0-6-0, No. 65462, stands at Sheringham, North Norfolk Railway, in September 1978.
Eric Sawford

Railway of origin Great Eastern Railway
Introduced 1883
Designer T.W. Worsdell (locos modified by J. Holden)
Purpose Light mixed traffic
Wheel arrangement 0-6-0
Driving wheel diameter 4 ft 11 in
Cylinders Two (inside) 17½ in by 24 in
Tractive effort 16,940 lb
Number built 289

For many decades, these classic Great Eastern Railway light mixed traffic engines were such a familiar sight both on branch lines in East Anglia and the suburbs of East London that they almost became part of the landscape. Like many other venerable classes of smaller locomotives, the 'J15s' (known as 'Y14s' in GER days) were so perfectly suited to the duties they undertook and the lines on which they ran (with endearing qualities such as ruggedness, economy and simplicity) that there was no reason to replace them with anything else. Even as late as 1959, no fewer than forty were still on British Railways' books. Happily, a single example, No. 65462, still survives in the authentic surroundings of the North Norfolk Railway.

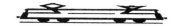

Midland 'Spinner'

Midland Railway 'Spinner' No. 673 steams proudly in the Rainhill
Cavalcade on 25 May 1980.
R. C. Riley

Railway of origin Midland Railway
Introduced 1887
Designer Samuel Waite Johnson
Purpose Express passenger
Wheel arrangement 4-2-2
Driving wheel diameter 7 ft 4½ in to 7 ft 9½ in,
depending on variant
Cylinders Two (inside) 18 in x 26 in, 18½ in x 26 in, or
19 in x 26 in, depending on variant
Tractive effort approx 14,500 lb to 15,000 lb
Number built 95

There was a grace and beauty about the 'single
wheelers', as they were known, which put them in a
class apart, and Johnson's 4-2-2 racehorses of the
Midland Railway were among the finest of their
breed. A single pair of large-diameter driving wheels
always gave the advantage of low friction and rapid
performance, but sufferered the disadvantage of low
traction, particularly upon starting. The tendency of
the driving wheels to spin gave these engines the
nickname of 'Spinners', even though steam-blast
sanding gear was used to regain grip. The last
'Spinner' in service, No. 673, was saved by the
LMS and still survives in the National Collection.

'*J36*' 0-6-0

No. 673 'Maude' positively gleams at the head of a main line steam special.
Chris Milner

Railway of origin North British Railway
Introduced 1888
Designer Matthew Holmes
Purpose Goods
Wheel arrangement 0-6-0
Driving wheel diameter 5ft 0 in
Cylinders Two (inside) 18¼ in x 26 in
Tractive effort 19,690 lb
Number built 168

From humble beginnings as a general purpose goods
engine, No. 673 'Maude' is the sole surviving
member of Matthew Holmes' once numerous 'C'
class 0-6-0s built for Scotland's North British
Railway between 1888 and 1900, and has become
much celebrated as a consistent performer on main
line steam specials. Fully restored and owned by the
Scottish Railway Preservation Society, its moment
of glory came when it travelled all the way from
Scotland to Rainhill under its own steam to take part
in the big 'Rocket 150' parade in 1980. During the
First World War, twenty-five of these locomotives
were sent abroad, and when they returned names
such as 'Ypres', 'Ole Bill', 'Somme' and so on were
bestowed on them. 'Maude' (BR No. 65243) was one
of these, and was still in British Railways' service
along with eighty-five others in the late 1950s.

Lancashire & Yorkshire Class '27' 0-6-0

No. 1300 evokes memories of another age at Steamtown, Carnforth
Chris Milner

Railway of origin Lancashire & Yorkshire Railway
Introduced 1889
Designer John A.F. Aspinall
Purpose Goods
Wheel arrangement 0-6-0
Driving wheel diameter 5 ft 1 in
Cylinders Two (inside) 18 in x 26 in
Tractive effort 21,130 lb
Number built 400-plus

Even in the late 1950s and early 1960s, some steam
locomotive designs dating from well before the turn
of the century were still at work on Britain's railways,
even though these had often been rebuilt in a
number of ways. One such class was the Lancashire
& Yorkshire Railway's faithful class '27' inside-
cylinder 0-6-0s, which were the mainstay of that
railway's freight operations. Designed by the L&Y
Locomotive Superintendent John A.F. Aspinall, and
introduced as long ago as 1889, they were still at work
well into British Railways days, centred around their
original area of operation but also to be seen at other
places on the London Midland Region. The sole
survivor, No. 1300 (BR No. 52322), built at Horwich
in 1896, can be found at Steamtown, Carnforth.

'T9' 4-4-0

'T9' No. 30719 at Padstow on 15 July 1960.
R.C. Riley

Railway of origin London & South Western Railway
Introduced 1899
Designer Dugald Drummond
Purpose Passenger
Wheel arrangement 4-4-0
Driving wheel diameter 6ft 7 in
Cylinders Two (inside) 19 in x 26 in
Tractive effort 17,675 lb
Number built 60-plus

The elegent 'T9' 4-4-0s, introduced to the London
& South Western Railway just before the turn of the
century, were among Britain's truly classic steam
locomotive designs, and some of them were still
serving British Railways sixty years later.
Distinguished by their rimless 'stovepipe'
chimneys, generally rakish lines and eight-wheeled
tenders, they worked most express traffic over the
difficult LSWR main line from Salisbury to Exeter
for many years, until larger locomotives took over,
and fully earned their nickname of 'Greyhounds'.
Even in the latter years of BR steam, more than a
dozen were still employed on semi-fast passenger
services. Happily a single survivor, No. 30120, is
retained in the National Collection and can be seen
at the Mid-Hants Railway.

'City' 4-4-0

The preserved 'City of Truro' pictured at Reading.
R.C. Riley

Railway of origin Great Western Railway
Introduced 1903
Designer George Jackson Churchward (development of
Dean design with taper boiler and Belpaire firebox)
Purpose Express passenger
Wheel arrangement 4-4-0
Driving wheel diameter 6 ft 8½ in
Cylinders Two (inside) 18 in x 26 in
Tractive effort 17,790 lb
Number built 10

Reputed to be the first locomotive in Britain to
exceed 100 mph as long ago as 1904, No. 3440
(later 3717) 'City of Truro' quickly established a place in
railway folklore and was set aside for preservation by
the Great Western Railway when it was withdrawn
from service as No. 3717 in 1931. It went to the
original York Railway Museum, and in 1957 it was
recommissioned for special main-line duties. It later
passed to the Swindon Railway Museum, and
remains an important item in the National
Collection, still venturing out on the main line from
time to time. Some say the speed hit by No. 3440
while heading an Ocean Mails special near
Wellington in May 1904 was as high as 102.3 mph,
but the authenticity of this has remained the subject
of great debate for many years.

'4F' 0-6-0

Midland '4F' No. 43924 eases coaching stock away from Keighley in 1981.
Chris Milner

Railway of origin Midland Railway
Introduced 1911
Designer Henry Fowler
Purpose Freight
Wheel arrangement 0-6-0
Driving wheel diameter 5 ft 3 in
Cylinders Two (inside) 20 in x 26 in
Tractive effort 24,555 lb
Number built 770-plus (including LMS-built examples)

One of the most numerous classes to be found on the London Midland Region of British Railways, and with a history stretching back to 1911, the Midland '4F' 0-6-0s and their London Midland & Scottish Railway-built counterparts numbered more than 770 examples. In the industrial North and Midlands they were used for a large number of goods and shunting duties, and it was not uncommon to see them at work on local passenger services as well. Some of them were built for the Somerset & Dorset Railway, on which system they remained for many years. The very first steam locomotive to be rescued from Barry Scrapyard was a '4F', No. 43924, the only Midland Railway-built example left, which is now at the Keighley & North Valley Railway.

Robinson 2-8-0

No. 63870 stands at New England Shed, Peterborough, on 31 May 1958.
R. C. Riley

Railway of origin Great Central Railway
Introduced 1911
Designer J.G. Robinson
Purpose Heavy freight
Wheel arrangement 2-8-0
Driving wheel diameter 4 ft 8 in
Cylinders Two (outside) 21 in x 26 in
Tractive effort 31,325 lb
Number built 500-plus

The Great Central Railway's standard heavy freight design, built from 1911 onwards, became a true classic, and distinguished itself by being chosen by the Government for service abroad during the First World War. In addition to the 130 built for the GCR, hundreds more were produced for the war effort, and when large numbers returned to Britain they were taken up by other railways, including the Great Western and London & North Western. They plodded on for many years, mostly on the London & North Eastern Railway which eventually had more than 400, rebuilding many of them into several variants with new boilers and so on. The '04s' (LNER classification) and their descendants were still hard at work on several parts of the system in the 1950s and early 1960s.

Somerset & Dorset 2-8-0

Restored to LMS black livery, Somerset & Dorset '7F' No. 13809 (BR No. 53809) explodes into action with an enthusiasts' special.
Chris Milner

Railway of origin Somerset & Dorset Joint Railway
Introduced 1914
Designer Sir Henry Fowler
Purpose Freight
Wheel arrangement 2-8-0
Driving wheel diameter 4 ft 8½ in
Cylinders Two (outside) 21 in x 28 in
Tractive effort 35,295 lb
Number built 11

These large-cylindered 2-8-0s were designed by Sir Henry Fowler of the Midland Railway, the company which had joint responsibility with the London & South Western Railway for the provision of locomotives for the Somerset & Dorset Line. They were built specifically to handle – without assistance – that route's considerable freight traffic, which included heavy coal and stone. The first four were built at Derby Works, and the remaining five slightly enlarged versions (ordered by the London Midland & Scottish Railway after the 1923 grouping) at Robert Stephenson & Co. Darlington. Bigger than anything previously produced by the Midland Railway, the '7Fs' as they became known were so ideally suited to conditions on the Somerset & Dorset line that they remained faithful to the route all their lives.

'U' Class (Ireland)

'U' class 4-4-0 No. 202 'Louth' stands at Clones with a Dublin-Enniskillen train in April 1956.
T.J. Edgington/Colour-Rail

Railway of origin Great Northern Railway (Ireland)
Introduced 1915
Designer G.T. Glover
Purpose Passenger
Wheel arrangement 4-4-0
Driving wheel diameter 5 ft 9 in
Cylinders Two (inside) 18 in x 24 in
Tractive effort 16,763 lb
Number built 10

These elegent 4-4-0s were so ideally suited to their role as medium-powered passenger locomotives working mainly on services out of Belfast that the first five, built by Beyer Peacock & Co as long ago as 1915, were supplemented by five more in 1947. At that time, with nationalisation around the corner on the British mainland, it was unusual to see such a basic Edwardian design being perpetuated, and this final batch became the last inside-cylinder 4-4-0s to be built in the world. Their classic lines looked their best in the sky blue livery of the Great Northern Railway (Ireland) seen in the accompanying photograph. Even as late as the mid-1960s, surviving members of this celebrated class could still be found on local passenger trains.

'King Arthur' 4-6-0

No. 777 'Sir Lamiel', in typical immaculate condition, on 'Cumbrian Mountain Pullman' duty.
Chris Milner

Railway of origin London & South Western Railway
Introduced 1918
Designer R.W. Urie
Purpose Express passenger
Wheel arrangement 4-6-0
Driving wheel diameter 6 ft 7 in
Cylinders Two (outside) 22 in x 28 in, later modified
Tractive effort 26,245 lb
Number built 74

One of the most rugged and reliable locomotives ever built for services in the south of England, with a pedigree stretching back to the London & South Western Railway in 1918, the 'King Arthur' 4-6-0s were produced in several distinct batches, and were improved even further by small design modifications as time went on. They bore romantic names such as 'Maid of Astolat', 'Morgan le Fay' and 'The Red Knight', and were happy both on boat trains from London Victoria to Dover and heavy trains on the Southern main line to Exeter from Basingstoke. After Urie's prototype design, 'King Arthurs' developed by R.E.L. Maunsell began appearing in quantity in 1925, and the sole survivor today, the National Railway Museum's No. 777 (BR No. 30777) 'Sir Lamiel', is one of these.

'Big Bertha'

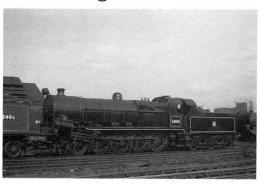

*The Lickey banking engine 'Big Bertha' with its BR number of 58100
stands ex-works at Derby in lined-out BR black livery.*
E. Oldham/Colour-Rail

Railway of origin Midland Railway
Introduced 1919
Designer Henry Fowler
Purpose Banking duties
Wheel arrangement 0-10-0
Driving wheel diameter 4 ft 7½ in
Cylinders Four (two outside, two inside) 16¾ in x 28 in
Tractive effort 43,315 lb
Number built 1

Designed for one purpose only – the banking (or
pushing) of trains up the formidable 1 in 37.5
gradient between Bromsgrove and Blackwell – the
unique four-cylinder Lickey banking engine, known
affectionately as 'Big Bertha', was the largest
locomotive built by the Midland Railway, and could
put down a huge (by British standards) tractive effort
of 43,315 lb. For more than three decades, its duties
never varied. It would wait beside the former Midland
Railway's main line from the West to the heart of the
Midlands, its footplate crew carefully tending the
fire for the mighty effort to come. A train requiring
assistance would arrive, and after an exchange of
whistles, 'Big Bertha' would go flat-out pushing it
over the three miles to the top before easing off and
coasting back down the hill for the next short,
sharp, but nevertheless extremely taxing duty.

'Large Director' 4-4-0

The sole-surviving 'Large Director', No. 506 'Butler-Henderson', at the Great Central Railway.
Chris Milner

Railway of origin Great Central Railway
Introduced 1920
Designer J.G. Robinson
Purpose Express passenger
Wheel arrangement 4-4-0
Driving wheel diameter 6 ft 9 in
Cylinders Two (inside) 20 in x 26 in
Tractive effort 19,645 lb
Number built 11 (plus 24 'D11/2s' for Scotland)

One of the Great Central Railway's classic designs, classified 'D11/1' when that railway became part of the London & North Eastern Railway in 1923, the 'Large Directors' were a 1920 development of the original ten 1913-built 'Directors'. They were intended for express passenger services on which their 6 ft 9 in driving wheels gave them a good turn of speed. Later in their careers they were drafted to lighter duties, including Liverpool Central-Manchester Central commuter trains and, on occasion, goods trains. No. 506 'Butler-Henderson' (BR No. 62660) is now part of the national collection, and after a long spell on loan to the Great Central Railway, Loughborough, it appeared briefly in British Railways' Black livery early in 1992.

'G2' 0-8-0

No. 49106 pictured at Berkhamsted in 1962.
R.C. Riley

Railway of origin London & North Western Railway
Introduced 1921
Designer Charles John Bowen-Cooke
Purpose Heavy freight
Wheel arrangement 0-8-0
Driving wheel diameter 4 ft 5½ in
Cylinders Two (inside) 20½ in x 24 in
Tractive effort 28,045 lb
Number built 60 (in addition to 250-plus G2a locos of broadly similar design)

The London & North Western Railway's prime freight class, the first versions of which were introduced under Francis William Webb in 1892, the superheated 'G2' 0-8-0s were the final development of a long and successful line. Built to handle long and heavy trains weighing up to 900 tons, many of them lasted into the 1960s. When working hard, they had a distinctive 'Chuff! CHUFF! Chuff! Wheeze!' rhythm which endeared them to enthusiasts. Sturdily built, and able to take all kinds of abuse, they were even used occasionally on holiday excursion trains and for emergency passenger duties, on which they could run at almost 60 mph! For such an important and long lived class, it is deplorable that only one – No. 9395 (BR 49395) – still exists, restored only cosmetically.

'Castle' 4-6-0

*No. 5051 'Drysllwyn Castle' on home territory near London
Paddington during the 'GWR 150' celebrations in 1985.*
Chris Milner

Railway of origin Great Western Railway
Introduced 1923
Designer C.B. Collett
Purpose Express passenger
Wheel Arrangement 4-6-0
Driving wheel diameter 6 ft 8½ in
Cylinders Four (two outside, two inside) 16 in x 26 in
Tractive effort 31,625 lb
Number built 171

Perhaps the most beautifully proportioned of all the
Great Western Railway's revered express passenger
locomotive classes, the four-cylinder 'Castle' 4-6-0s
were basically an enlargement under C.B. Collett,
the GWR's Chief Mechanical Engineer, of George
Jackson Churchward's 'Star' 4-6-0s. Fast and
powerful, working crack turns such as 'Cheltenham
Flyer' (on which No. 5006 'Tregenna Castle' made a
non-stop run from Swindon to London Paddington
at an average of 81.6 mph in 1932) they were capable
of 100 mph, with their 6 ft 9½ in driving wheels
enabling high speeds to be kept up over long
distances. The 'Castles' eventually numbered 171.
Pioneer No. 4073 'Caerphilly Castle' is now at the
Science Museum, South Kensington, and eight
'Castles' are still with us, one of them, No. 4079
'Pendennis Castle', in Australia. Others such as
Nos. 5080 'Defiant' and 7029 'Clun Castle', still
make occasional main-line forays.

'Hall' 4-6-0

No. 4930 'Hagley Hall' in typically superb condition at an enthusiasts' day at the Severn Valley Railway.
Chris Milner

Railway of origin Great Western Railway
Introduced 1924 (prototype), 1928 (remainder)
Designer C.B. Collett
Purpose Mixed traffic
Wheel arrangement 4-6-0
Driving wheel diameter 6ft 0 in
Cylinders Two (outside) 18½ in x 30 in
Tractive effort 27,275 lb
Number built 329

The Great Western Railway's premier mixed traffic
locomotives were the 'Hall' 4-6-0s built between
1923 and 1943. The original 'Hall', No. 4900, was a
rebuild of one of G.J. Churchward's 'Saint' 4-6-0s,
and retained its name 'Saint Martin'. More than 250
versions of the 4900, 5900 and 6900 series and a
further 71 of the 6959 and 7900 'Modified Hall'
series were built, and the GWR had problems in
finding enough names to go round! They could be
found as far apart as Chester and Penzance, and
were equally at home on fast milk or fitted freight
services as they were on passenger trains. Always
lively performers, the 'Halls' were often praised by
footplate crew, and fortunately the locomotives'
distinctive sharp bark can still be heard today.
Preserved examples include Nos 4920 'Dumbleton
Hall', 4930 'Hagley Hall', 4983 'Albert Hall', 5900
'Hinderton Hall', and 5952 'Cogan Hall'.

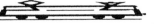

'Jinty' 0-6-0 Tank

'Jinty' No. 47279 in charge of a demonstration goods train at the Keighley & Worth Valley Railway.
Chris Milner

Railway of origin London Midland & Scottish Railway
Introduced 1924
Designer Henry Fowler
Purpose Light shunting, pilot and local duties
Wheel arrangement 0-6-0
Driving wheel diameter 4 ft 7 in
Cylinders Two (inside) 18 in x 26 in
Tractive effort 20,835 lb
Number built 400-plus

Based on a Midland Railway design of 1899, the '3F' or 'Jinty' 0-6-0 tank engines were all built for the London Midland & Scottish Railway, and they eventually numbered almost 420. They could be found at many stations and in goods yards all over what became the London Midland Region of British Railways, often simmering away in bay platforms or busying themselves as station pilots, undertaking many of the duties which were to continue with their successors, the class '08' diesel electric 0-6-0s. Some 'Jinties' remain active in preservation, the best known of them including No. 47279 at the Keighley & Worth Valley Railway and No. 47383 at the Severn Valley Railway. Others can be found at the Midland Railway Centre, Butterley, and the Llangollen Railway.

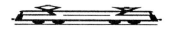

'P1' 2-8-2

No. 2393 on display at New Barnet in a coat of extremely glossy black paint in 1937.
Colour-Rail

Railway of origin London & North Eastern Railway
Introduced 1925
Designer Sir Nigel Gresley
Purpose Heavy freight
Wheel arrangement 2-8-2
Driving wheel diameter 5 ft 2 in
Cylinders Three (two outside, one inside) 19 in x 26 in
Tractive effort 42,460 lb
Number built 2

Such was Sir Nigel Gresley's flair for design that when a pair of ultra-powerful freight locomotives were required for hauling 100-wagon coal trains weighing 1,500 tons and more between Peterborough and London, the 'P1' 2-8-2s which resulted did not look like goods engines at all, but sleek black beauties resembling express passenger locomotives in everything except their small driving wheels – which is exactly what they were! One of them, No. 2394, was even tried on passenger service along its normal route and kept up 65 mph easily. When their original 180 lb boilers were replaced by 220 lb ones, the tractive effort of the 'P1s' grew from 38,500 (enhanced by a booster in original form) to an impressive 42,460 lb. After twenty years of service, Nos. 2393/4 were withdrawn, although their boilers lived on in 'A3' 'Pacifics'.

LNER Beyer-Garratt

No. 69999 heads a freight train from Dewsnap up towards Dunford Bridge on the former Great Central line in 1955, its final year of operation.
E. Oldham/Colour-Rail

Railway of origin London & North Eastern Railway
Introduced 1925
Designer Beyer Peacock/Sir Nigel Gresley
Purpose Very heavy freight
Wheel arrangement 2-8-8-2T
Driving wheel diameter 4 ft 8 in
Cylinders Six (four outside, two inside) 18½ in x 26 in
Tractive effort 72,940 lb
Number built 1

Easily the most powerful steam locomotive to run in Britain, with a staggering tractive effort of 72,940 lb, the LNER Beyer-Garratt, No. 9999 (BR No. 69999) was built for the haulage and banking of heavy goods trains around Wath. Electrification of the first part of the Manchester-Sheffield-Wath Woodhead route (from Wath to Dunford Bridge) at 1,500 V dc in 1952 brought a revision of the giant locomotive's duties, and for a spell it worked on the Midland Railway's Lickey incline as a replacement for the 0-10-0 'Big Bertha'. Towards the end of its life, No. 69999 was converted into an oil-burning locomotive, in which form it is seen in this photograph. It was finally broken up in 1955.

'N2' 0-6-2 Tank

*The sole preserved 'N2', No. 4744, runs into Loughborough, Great
Central Railway, with a train from Rothley in August 1981.*
Chris Milner

Railway of origin London & North Eastern Railway
Introduced 1925
Designer Sir Nigel Gresley
Purpose Suburban passenger
Wheel arrangement 0-6-2
Driving wheel diameter 5 ft 8 in
Cylinders Two (inside) 19 in x 26 in
Tractive effort 19,945 lb
Number built 100-plus

Once upon a time, it would have been impossible to
imagine the former Great Northern main line
leading out of King's Cross without the busy sights
and sounds of these famous little locomotives
scurrying to and fro on densely packed local
commuter services, often with destination boards
attached to their smokebox doors. Now, alas, only a
single example remains, No. 4744 (later BR
No. 69523), at the Great Central Railway,
Loughborough. Originally designed for the Great
Northern Railway by Sir Nigel Gresley, and later
developed for the London & North Eastern
Railway, the 'N2s' featured a short, stubby chimney
to comply with the Metropolitan Railway's loading
gauge on Moorgate services, and many had
condensing gear allowing them to operate better in
tunnelled parts of London.

'N7' 0-6-2T

'N7' 0-6-2T No. 69621, built at Stratford, East London, in 1924,
attends an open day at Cambridge.
E.H. Sawford

Railway of origin London & North Eastern Railway
(from original Great Eastern Railway design)
Introduced 1925
Designer A.J. Hill, Great Eastern Railway
Purpose Suburban passenger and pilot duties
Wheel arrangement 0-6-2T
Driving wheel diameter 4 ft 10 in
Cylinders Two (inside) 18 in x 24 in
Tractive effort 20,515 lb
Number built 134

The handsome 'N7' tank locomotives were
developed from a Great Eastern Railway design by
A.J. Hill dating from 1915, and they worked on
outer surburban services from London's Liverpool
Street Station. Over the years, several detail
alterations were made to the original classic design,
although the various sub-classes always retained a
GER look. One 'N7', No. 694, was kept in
superb condition as a Liverpool Street pilot,
alongside 'J69' 0-6-0T No. 68619. Many 'N7s' were
rebuilt with round-topped boilers and the sole
surviving example, No. 69621, was one of these.
Recently restored, it is kept immaculately, bringing
back memories of the glory of steam at Liverpool
Street. It is no stranger to railway open days, where
it is always greatly admired.

'Lord Nelson' 4-6-0

*Restored in Southern Railway malachite green, No. 850 'Lord Nelson'
makes a fine sight at Steamtown, Carnforth, in the early 1980s.*
Chris Milner

Railway of origin Southern Railway
Introduced 1926
Designer R.E.L. Maunsell
Purpose Heavy express passenger
Wheel arrangement 4-6-0
Driving wheel diameter 6 ft 7 in
Cylinders Four (two outside, two inside) 16½ in x 26 in
Tractive effort 33,510 lb
Number built 16

A unique feature of the sixteen 'Lord Nelson' 4-6-0s
introduced by R.E.L. Maunsell for the Southern
Railway in 1926 was that their mechanical design in
setting the cranks at 135° produced no fewer than
eight individual exhaust blasts for each rotation of
their driving wheels compared with the normal four
for both two and four-cylinder designs. This gave
them surefooted starting on the heavy boat trains
from London Waterloo to Southampton for which
they were principally intended, and they could
capably haul trains weighing as much as 500 tons.
Originally designed with small single chimneys, the
locomotives were later considerably modified by
O.V.S. Bulleid, receiving multiple-jet blastpipes
and much wider chimneys. The locomotives were
named after great naval commanders and the
original, No. 850 'Lord Nelson' (BR No. 30850),
has been preserved in the National Collection.

'Crab' 2-6-0

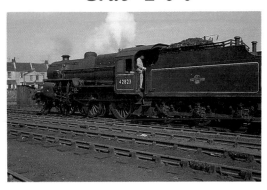

No. 42823 at Bristol (Barrow Road) on 5 July 1959.
R.C. Riley

Railway of origin London Midland & Scottish Railway
Introduced 1926
Designer George Hughes
Purpose Mixed traffic
Wheel arrangement 2-6-0
Driving wheel diameter 5 ft 6 in
Cylinders Two (outside) 21 in x 26 in
Tractive effort 26,580 lb
Number built 245

Known as 'Horwich Moguls' or, more popularly, 'Crabs', the Hughes-designed mixed traffic 2-6-0s were notable for their large outside cylinders which, together with their relatively small diameter driving wheels, necessitated a pronounced raising of the running plate towards the front of the locomotive. When introduced for the LMS, these distinctive and capable engines were painted in LMS dark red, with large numbers on their tenders, but later they were finished in black, carrying lined mixed traffic livery in British Railways days. Powerful and free-running, the 'Crabs' were just as happy on heavy freight trains as they were on passenger excursions, and were particularly respected in the Ayrshire coalfield, where they put in some sterling work on heavy trains. The first 'Crab', No. 42700, remains in the National Collection and another, No. 42765, is at the Keighley & Worth Valley Railway.

'A3' 'Pacific'

'Flying Scotsman' makes a fine sight beneath York Station's curving roof with a 'Scarborough Spa Express' steam special.
Chris Milner

Railway of origin London & North Eastern Railway
Introduced 1927
Designer Sir Nigel Gresley
Purpose Express passenger
Wheel arrangement 4-6-2
Driving wheel diameter 6 ft 8 in
Cylinders Three (two outside, one inside) 19 in x 26 in
Tractive effort 32,910 lb
Number built 78

It is a sad fluke of history that while only one of the Gresley-designed three-cylinder 'A3' 'Pacific' locomotives of the London & North Eastern Railway survives today, that locomotive, No. 4472 'Flying Scotsman', is probably the most famous steam locomotive in the world. The 'A3s', which were virtually all named after racehorses such as 'Spearmint', 'Robert the Devil', 'Pretty Polly' and 'Captain Cuttle', were well capable of running at speeds in the 100 mph region, and headed many top expresses along the East Coast Main Line from King's Cross to Edinburgh. In 1935, No. 2750 (BR No. 60096) 'Papyrus' attained 108 mph on a special run from Newcastle-upon-Tyne to London. In preservation 'Flying Scotsman' (BR No. 60103) broke the long-distance record for steam during an Australian tour in 1988/9.

'King' 4-6-0

The magnificent No. 6000 'King George V' simmers in the morning sun at Didcot Railway Centre during the summer of 1983.
Chris Milner

Railway of origin Great Western Railway
Introduced 1927
Designer C.B. Collett
Purpose Heavy express passenger
Wheel arrangement 4-6-0
Driving wheel diameter 6 ft 6 in
Cylinders Four (two outside, two inside) 16¼ in x 28 in
Tractive effort 40,285 lb
Number built 30

The 'Kings' were the most powerful 4-6-0s ever built in Britain, and epitomised the glory of the Great Western Railway, on which their capabilities at the head of huge and heavily loaded express passenger trains became legendary. Designed by C.B. Collett and built between 1927 and 1930, the thirty examples of the class were utilised on crack duties such as the 'Cornish Riviera Express' and 'Bristolian', as well as the major Paddington to Birmingham/Wolverhampton passenger turns. Their route availability was classified as 'double red', which meant their very high axle-loading restricted their sphere of operation to a small number of specified routes. Three 'Kings' live on today; No. 6000 'King George V' (pictured), No. 6023 'King Edward II' and No. 6024 'King Edward I', the latter cleared for main line running.

'S15' 4-6-0

In plain black BR freight livery, S15 No. 30500, on 18 May 1963.
R.C. Riley

Railway of origin Southern Railway
Introduced 1927
Designer R.E.L. Maunsell
Purpose Mixed traffic, mostly freight
Wheel arrangement 4-6-0
Driving wheel diameter 5 ft 7 in
Cylinders Two (outside) 20½ in x 28 in
Tractive effort 29,855 lb
Number built 45

The powerful 'S15' 4-6-0s were given a '6F'
(freight) power classification under British Railways
ownership, and the final survivors in BR service
were at Feltham where there were extensive goods
sidings. Like some other Southern Railway designs,
batches were constructed with detail differences.
The first twenty, Nos. 30496-30515, were developed
from the London & South Western Railway's 'N15'
4-6-0s by R.W. Urie. These had a boiler pressure of
180 lb, 21 in x 28 in cylinders and a tractive effort of
28,200 lb. A second batch of fifteen, built under
Maunsell from 1927 onwards, had 200 lb boiler
pressure and slightly smaller cylinders, giving a
higher tractive effort of 29,855 lb. These were
numbered 30823-30837 under BR.

LMS Beyer-Garratt

The rotary coal bunker of Beyer-Garratt No. 47981 can be seen clearly as the locomotive stands at Cricklewood Shed in May 1955.
T.B. Owen/Colour-Rail

Railway of origin London Midland & Scottish Railway
Introduced 1927
Designer Beyer Peacock/Sir Henry Fowler
Purpose Very heavy freight
Wheel arrangement 2-6-6-2T
Driving wheel diameter 5 ft 3 in
Cylinders Four (all outside) 18½ in x 26 in
Tractive effort 45,620 lb
Number built 33

The London Midland & Scottish Railway's Beyer-Garratt design was smaller than the LNER's mighty No. 9999, but no fewer than thirty-three examples were built to handle the heavy coal traffic which was generated in the vast marshalling yards at Toton, near Nottingham and transported to Cricklewood in London for distribution all over the capital. The Beyer-Garratts, which were really two engines in one, were also common visitors to Peterborough. The first examples, introduced in 1927, had fixed coal bunkers, but the modified versions which followed from 1930 onwards were eventually fitted with revolving bunkers, which made the hard-pressed footplate crew's duties that much easier. With a decline of the rail-borne trade in coal for general distribution and the emergence of simpler types such as the BR 9F 2-10-0s, the LMS Beyer-Garratts disappeared one by one.

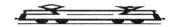

'Large Prairie' Tank

'Large Prairie' No. 5164 stands near a water tower at its home, the Severn Valley Railway.
Chris Milner

Railway of origin Great Western Railway
Introduced 1928, as development of 1906 design
Designer C.B. Collett, as development of George Jackson Churchward design
Purpose Medium-distance mixed traffic
Wheel arrangement 2-6-2T
Driving wheel diameter 5 ft 8 in
Cylinders Two (outside) 18 in x 30 in
Tractive effort 24,300 lb
Number built 194

Much of the Great Western Railway's branch and short to medium-distance passenger traffic was moved by a family of 2-6-2 or 'Prairie' tank engines which had been introduced as long ago as 1906 under the great George Jackson Churchward, and subsequently developed by his successor, C.B. Collett. In both 'Large' and 'Small' versions, the 'Prairies' were supremely modern for their time, and were noted for their crisp power and strong acceleration. Not surprisingly, many survivors are still active at preserved railways today, no fewer than twenty-three of several varieties having been rescued from Barry Scrapyard. Among the most useful all-round locomotives the GWR possessed, the 'Prairies' were still being built into early nationalisation years.

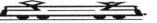

'5700' Class Pannier Tank

'5700' class 0-6-0 pannier tank No. 7760 at Woodthorpe, Great Central Railway.
Chris Milner

Railway of origin Great Western Railway
Introduced 1929
Designer C.B. Collett
Purpose Light general duties
Wheel arrangement 0-6-0PT
Driving wheel diameter 4 ft 7½ in
Cylinders Two (inside) 17½ in x 24 in
Tractive effort 22,515 lb
Number built 850-plus

These ubiquitous little tank engines were once a common sight all over the former Great Western Railway system on light goods, light passenger and shunting duties. Their development goes back to 1897 with William Dean's saddle tank locomotives. These were subsequently rebuilt as pannier tanks, setting a GWR trend that would last for many years. London Transport bought a batch between 1953 and 1963 to replace older Metropolitan locomotives for shunting duties. No fewer than sixteen pannier tanks survive in preservation, at venues ranging from the Dean Forest Railway to the Keighley & Worth Valley Railway and the Llangollen Railway.

'U' Class 2-6-0

'U' class 2-6-0 No. 31626 heads its passenger train past 'West Country'
'Pacific' No. 34041 'Wilton' – on lowly shunting duties! – at Yeovil
Junction on 10 July 1959.
R.C. Riley

Railway of origin Southern Railway (first 20 examples
rebuilt from South Eastern & Chatham Railway 'River'
class 2-6-4 tank locomotives)
Introduced 1928
Designer R.E.L. Maunsell
Purpose Mixed traffic
Wheel arrangement 2-6-0
Driving wheel diameter 6 ft 0 in
Cylinders Two (outside) 19 in x 28 in. Three (two outside,
one inside) 16 in x 28 in ('U1' class only)
Tractive effort 23,865 lb ('U1 25,385 lb)
Number built 71

One of the Southern Railway's most successful
mixed traffic locomotive designs, the first twenty
'Us' were rebuilt as straightforward two-cylinder
2-6-0s from the powerful but unstable 'River' class
passenger tank locomotives which themselves had
been introduced on the South Eastern & Chatham
Railway in 1917. Thirty more 'Us' were built as new
two-cylinder engines with detail differences from
the first batch, bringing the class total up to fifty. A
further twenty-one, classified 'U1', had three
cylinders and a correspondingly higher tractive
effort. All three types were to be found on a wide
variety of mixed traffic duties.

'Patriot' 4-6-0

No. 45506 'The Royal Pioneer Corps' at Bristol (Barrow Road) on 5 July 1959. In the background is a former Great Western 2-6-0.
R.C. Riley

Railway of origin London Midland & Scottish Railway
Introduced Two in 1930; remainder from 1933, with rebuilds from 1946
Designer Sir Henry Fowler
Purpose Express passenger
Wheel arrangement 4-6-0
Driving wheel diameter 6 ft 9 in
Cylinders Three (two outside, one inside) 18 in x 26 in (rebuilds 17 in x 26 in with higher boiler pressure)
Tractive effort 26,520 lb (rebuilds 29,570 lb)
Number built 52

The first two 'Baby Scot' 4-6-0s were rebuilt from London & North Western Railway 'Claughton' 4-6-0s, but the rest, built from 1933 onwards, were new locomotives. The class became known as 'Patriots' after the elaborate nameplate fitted to the first locomotive, No. 45500 'Patriot'. With their small chimneys and large-diameter driving wheels, they had a powerful although somewhat gawky appearance, and were renowned for the towering pillars of black smoke they could produce. They were well-respected by the locomotive crews who worked them on a large variety of express trains throughout the London Midland area. 'Patriots' were named mostly after British regiments and holiday resorts in the north west and north Wales, although some remained nameless.

'Schools' 4-4-0

No. 30915 'Brighton' on a Ramsgate–London express at St Mary Cray Junction on 16 May 1959.
R. C. Riley

Railway of origin Southern Railway
Introduced 1930
Designer R.E.L. Maunsell
Purpose Express passenger
Wheel arrangement 4-4-0
Driving wheel diameter 6 ft 7 in
Cylinders Three (two outside, one inside) 16½ in x 26 in
Tractive effort 25,135 lb
Number built 40

The most powerful and successful 4-4-0s to run in Britain, and extremely nice-looking engines to boot, the 'Schools' 4-4-0s were conceived for service on the former South Eastern & Chatham Railway's Hastings line, where their narrow bodies were necessary because of extra linings that had to be built into tunnels on that difficult route. The 'Schools' could handle extremely heavy trains for their size – certainly of 400 tons and more – and were so successful that they were called on to undertake arduous duties to Portsmouth, Southampton, Bournemouth and other important main line centres as well. Although they were first built with narrow single chimneys, O.V.S. Bulleid (who succeeded Maunsell in 1937) rebuilt about half of the class with multiple-jet blastpipes and much wider chimneys. All were named after famous public schools.

'V' Class 4-4-0 (Ireland)

In its final form, GNR(I) 'V' class compound No. 86 'Peregrine'
brings an express into Amiens Street Station in June 1959.
A.G. Cramp/Colour-Rail

Railway of origin Great Northern Railway (Ireland)
Introduced 1932
Designer G.T. Glover
Purpose Express passenger
Wheel arrangement 4-4-0
Driving wheel diameter 6 ft 7 in
Cylinders Three (two outside, one inside) 17¼ in x 26 in (inside); 19 in x 26 in (outside)
Tractive effort 23, 760 lb (later reduced to 20,435 lb)
Number built 5

These five extremely powerful high-pressure 4-4-0 compounds were built by Beyer Peacock & Co. in 1932 for working express trains over Ireland's Great Northern main line between Belfast and Dublin, and were the last compound locomotives (in which steam is used twice) to be built in Britain. At first these locomotives, Nos. 83 'Eagle', 84 'Falcon', 85 'Merlin', 86 'Peregrine' and 87 'Kestrel' were built with round-topped boilers with a high working pressure of 250 lb per sq in, but these were eventually replaced by different boilers with square Belpaire fireboxes, and the pressure came down to 215 lb, reducing the tractive effort somewhat. One of the 'Vs', No. 85 'Merlin', lives on in preservation and can still be seen on Irish main line steam specials.

'Princess Royal'

'Princess Royal' 'Pacific' No. 46203 'Princess Margaret Rose',
sporting a 'Red Rose' (Euston–Liverpool) headboard, looks immaculate
shortly after its return to steam in 1990.
Chris Milner

Railway of origin London Midland & Scottish Railway
Introduced 1933
Designer Sir William A. Stanier
Purpose Heavy express passenger
Wheel arrangement 4-6-2
Driving wheel diameter 6 ft 6 in
Cylinders Four (two outside, two inside) 16¼ in x 28 in
Tractive effort 40,285 lb
Number built 13

The mighty 'Princess Royal' 'Pacifics' were built at
Crewe Works for handling extremely heavy
passenger trains unaided, particularly on intensively
used routes such as Euston-Liverpool and further
north, where Euston–Glasgow trains had to tackle
the formidable climbs to Shap and Beattock
summits. In November 1936 No. 6201 'Princess
Elizabeth', hauled an eight-coach test train from
London Euston to Glasgow and back, reaching 95
mph on each run and averaging 70 mph on the
return, thus paving the way for an accelerated
service. One of the class, No. 6202, was built as a
steam turbine locomotive in 1935. In 1952 it re-
emerged as a conventional locomotive and was
named 'Princess Anne', but tragically it was
destroyed in the Harrow & Wealdstone disaster after
only a few months' service in this guise.

Stanier 'Mogul'

Stanier 'Mogul' No. 42954 was photographed ex-works at Swindon in October 1964.
R.C. Riley

Railway of origin London Midland & Scottish Railway
Introduced 1933
Designer Sir William A. Stanier
Purpose Mixed traffic
Wheel arrangement 2-6-0
Driving wheel diameter 5 ft 6 in
Cylinders Two (outside) 18 in x 28 in
Tractive effort 26,290 lb
Number built 40

When Sir William A. Stanier went to the London Midland & Scottish Railway from the Great Western Railway in 1932, he took a number of sound Swindon practices with him, and some of these – such as a taper boiler (and at first even a GWR-style safety-valve bonnet!) – were incorporated into his first mixed-traffic 2-6-0 design for the LMS. These forty handsome locomotives, numbered from 2945 to 2984 (BR 42945 to 42984) followed on from the Hughes 'Crab' 2-6-0s, and were at home on a wide range of duties, principally freight and heavy excursion traffic, much as the 'Crabs'. A little shy of steam-raising at first, the Stanier 'Moguls' gave worthwhile if unspectacular service throughout their working lives, but were understandably eclipsed by Stanier's numerous 'Black Five' 4-6-0s which came out a year later. A single surviving 'Mogul', No. 42968, was rescued from Barry Scrapyard.

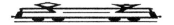
'Black Five' 4-6-0

Two 'Black Fives' are coaled at Carnforth, No. 4767 (BR No. 44767)
'George Stephenson' and Paddy Smith's celebrated No. 5407.
Chris Milner

Railway of origin London Midland & Scottish Railway
Introduced 1934
Designer Sir William A. Stanier
Purpose Mixed traffic
Wheel arrangement 4-6-0
Driving wheel diameter 6 ft 0 in
Cylinders Two (outside) 18½ in x 28 in
Tractive effort 25,455 lb
Number built 840-plus

The general-purpose, medium-power 'Black Five'
4-6-0s designed by Sir William A. Stanier for the
London Midland & Scottish Railway became one of
the most successful, probably *the* most successful,
mixed traffic locomotives of all time. With some 842
examples built, there was almost nothing a 'Black
Five' could not do, and they were a firm favourite
with footplate crew because of their economical
running and excellent power output. They were
built at many locomotive works, including Crewe,
Derby, Horwich, Vulcan Foundry and Armstrong
Whitworth, and many new features were tried out
on some of them including double chimneys,
Caprotti valve gear, Stephenson link motion and
different kinds of roller bearings. They were
involved in the operation of the final steam services
on British Railways in 1968, and some eighteen
examples escaped the cutting torch.

'Jubilee' 4-6-0

The double-chimneyed No.45596 'Bahamas' in superb condition at the Keighley & Worth Valley Railway.
Eric Sawford

Railway of origin London Midland & Scottish Railway
Introduced 1934
Designer Sir William A. Stanier
Purpose Express passenger
Wheel arrangement 4-6-0
Driving wheel diameter 6 ft 9 in
Cylinders Three (two outside, one inside) 17 in x 26 in
Tractive effort 26,610 lb
Number built 191

The first, 'Jubilee' 4-6-0, No. 5552, was named 'Silver Jubilee' in raised silver lettering to mark the twenty-fifth anniversary of King George V. The rest were named after countries in the British Empire – with almost a third of the world 'painted pink' in those days, there was no shortage of names – great naval commanders and warships. No fewer than 191 'Jubilees' were built, utilised all over LMS – later London Midland Region – territory on a wide variety of express passenger and fast freight duties. Their large driving wheels made them swift performers, and they made a particular impression on the Midland main line out of London St Pancras. A few were rebuilt with larger boilers and double chimneys to resemble closely the rebuilt 'Royal Scot' 4-6-0s. Of the survivors, No. 5596 (BR No. 45596) 'Bahamas' has a normal-sized boiler with a double chimney.

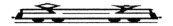

Stanier '8F'

One of the preserved Stanier '8F' locomotives, No. 48151, is based at the Midland Railway Centre, Butterley.
Chris Milner

Railway of origin London Midland & Scottish Railway
Introduced 1935
Designer Sir William A. Stanier
Purpose Heavy freight
Wheel arrangement 2-8-0
Driving wheel diameter 4 ft 8½ in
Cylinders Two (outside) 18½ in x 28 in
Tractive effort 32,440 lb
Number built 852

These rugged and powerful freight locomotives eventually numbered 852, of which 666 worked in Britain. They were built at several loco works including Crewe, North British (Glasgow), Darlington, Doncaster and Brighton. Many went abroad during the Second World War, and some were still working in the Middle East long after their British counterparts had been sent for scrap. Despite their relatively small driving wheel diameter, '8Fs' had a surprising turn of speed, and were often pressed into working holiday excursions. Towards the end of their lives, some '8Fs' carried a star below each cab-side number, indicating that balancing work had been carried out on them for working fast fitted freight trains. Happily, several '8Fs' live on in preservation, one having been 'liberated' from Turkey.

'*A4*' '*Pacific*'

'A4' 'Pacific' No. 4498 'Sir Nigel Gresley' stands at Weymouth Depot during a special visit on 4 June 1967.
Eric Sawford

Railway of origin London & North Eastern Railway
Introduced 1935
Designer Sir Nigel Gresley
Purpose Express passenger
Wheel arrangement 4-6-2
Driving wheel diameter 6 ft 8 in
Cylinders Three (two outside, one inside) 18½in x 26 in
(three locos had a 17 in x 26 in inside cylinder)
Tractive effort 35,455 lb (or 33,616 lb)
Number built 35

The streamlined 'A4' 'Pacifics' represented the zenith of Sir Nigel Gresley's genius as a designer of fast and efficient express passenger locomotives, and one example, No. 4468 'Mallard' (BR No. 60022), broke the world record for steam, attaining just over 126 mph during braking trials between Grantham and Peterborough in 1938. Even in everyday service, the 'Streaks', as they were nicknamed, could exceed 100 mph without difficulty, and often did. Survivors are Nos. 4498 (60007) 'Sir Nigel Gresley', 4496 (60008) 'Dwight D. Eisenhower' (in the USA), 4488 (60009) 'Union of South Africa', 4489 (60010) 'Dominion of Canada' (in Canada), 4464 (60019) 'Bittern', and, of course, 4468 (60022) 'Mallard'!

'Grange' 4-6-0

No. 6800 'Arlington Grange' at Stoneycombe sidings with a Penzance train in June 1958.
T.B. Owen/Colour-Rail

Railway of origin Great Western Railway
Introduced 1936
Designer C.B. Collett
Purpose Mixed traffic
Wheel arrangement 4-6-0
Driving wheel diameter 5 ft 8 in
Cylinders Two (outside) 18½ in x 30 in
Tractive effort 28,875 lb
Number built 80

One of the few types of Great Western main line
locomotives not to live on into preservation, the
'Grange' 4-6-0s were firm favourites with
footplatemen who knew there were few tasks these
fine mixed traffic engines could not tackle, up to and
including heavy passenger duties. Often described
as 'Halls' with smaller wheels, the 'Granges' utilised
some parts, such as driving wheels, from withdrawn
Churchward '4300' class 2-6-0s which had been
introduced in 1911. Recognised by stepped running
plates over their cylinders, the 'Granges' had 225 lb
per sq in boiler pressures and could be found all over
the GWR system, particularly in Cornwall where
they proved strong climbing engines. Under British
Railways, many were turned out in lined black
mixed traffic livery.

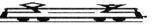

'Dukedog' 4-4-0

The only 'Dukedog' left, No. 3217 (later numbered 9017) 'Earl of Berkeley' on display at Didcot Steam Centre on 24 May 1985.
R.C. Riley

Railway of origin Great Western Railway
Introduced 1936 as rebuilds
Designer C.B.Collett (from original Dean locomotives)
Purpose Mixed traffic, primarily passenger
Wheel arrangement 4-4-0
Driving wheel diameter 5 ft 8 in
Cylinders Two (inside) 18 in x 26 in
Tractive effort 18,955 lb
Number built 30

The boilers of 'Duke' 4-4-0s introduced in 1895 and
the frames of 'Bulldog' 4-4-0s which made their first
appearance three years later were incorporated into
the 9000 class 'Dukedog' 4-4-0s which were put into
service between 1936 and 1939. Although they were
hybrids, the 'Dukedogs' continued the traditions of
the hardy and long-lived designs from which they
were evolved, even though they retained an antique
appearance with their outside frames and springs
and tall chimneys and domes. Nevertheless, these
willing locomotives put in some excellent work on
routes such as the Cambrian, and survived well into
the 1950s, a small number even managing to see out
the decade. The sole surviving 'Dukedog', No. 9017
'Earl of Berkeley', can be found at the Bluebell
Railway.

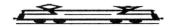

'V2' 2-6-2

No. 4771 'Green Arrow' pictured at Dinting Steam Centre.
Eric Sawford

Railway of origin London & North Eastern Railway
Introduced 1936
Designer Sir Nigel Gresley
Purpose Fast mixed traffic
Wheel arrangement 2-6-2
Driving wheel diameter 6 ft 2 in
Cylinders Three (two outside, one inside) 18½ in x 26 in
Tractive effort 33,730 lb
Number built 184

One of Sir Nigel Gresley's finest designs, with
examples still being built three years after his death
in 1941 from a heart attack at the age of 64, the 'V2'
2-6-2s were among the most beautifully
proportioned steam locomotives ever made, and
certainly one of the best mixed traffic designs to
grace Britain's railways. With performance almost
up to 'Pacific' standards, their wartime exploits
were legendary. The National Railway Museum's
excellent publication 'Gresley and Stanier' describes
how 'V2' No. 4800 hauled a gigantic train of twenty-
six coaches, weighing 850 tons with 1,300
passengers aboard, in 1940, and haulage of twenty
coach trains at speeds of 60 mph or so were well
within the capabilities of the 'V2s', or 'Green
Arrows' as they were known. With normal express
passenger loads, these sleek locomotives were well
up to sustained 80 to 90 mph running, and often
deputised for 'A3s' and 'A4s'.

'Coronation' 'Pacific'

*No. 46229 'Duchess of Hamilton' near Kirkby Stephen on a
'Cumbrian Mountain Express' over the Settle to Carlisle line.*
R. Jones/Colour-Rail

Railway of origin London Midland & Scottish Railway
Introduced 1937
Designer Sir William A. Stanier
Purpose Heavy express passenger
Wheel arrangement 4-6-2
Driving wheel diameter 6 ft 9 in
Cylinders Four (two outside, two inside) 16¼ in x 28 in
Tractive effort 40,000 lb
Number built 38

These celebrated 'Pacifics', the first of which were
streamlined and known officially as the 'Princess
Coronation' class, were among the most powerful
express passenger steam locomotives built in
Britain, and were capable of stirring haulage feats
with seventeen carriages or more in tow up the
formidable Shap and Beattock banks along the West
Coast Main Line from London Euston to Glasgow.
Under test, one of these fine machines produced
3,300 hp, although in everyday running this would
be limited by the capacity of the fireman to shovel in
enough coal to keep the huge boiler supplied with
steam! The first few examples came out with
Prussian blue streamlined casings to haul the
'Coronation Scot' prestige express. Several more
'streamliners' came out in maroon, and many were
never streamlined at all. In a record attempt, No.
6220 'Coronation' achieved 114 mph.

'W1' 4-6-4

In LNER garter blue livery, but carrying its 'British Railways' lettering on the tender, No. 60700 is caught at King's Cross shed in May 1951.
W.H.G. Boot/Colour-Rail

Railway of origin London & North Eastern Railway
Introduced 1937, as rebuild of experimental high-pressure water-tube four-cylinder compound No. 10000
Designer Sir Nigel Gresley
Purpose Heavy express passenger
Wheel arrangement 4-6-4
Driving wheel diameter 6 ft 8 in
Cylinders Three (two outside, one inside) 20 in x 26 in
Tractive effort 41,435 lb
Number built 1

At first glance resembling a nameless 'A4' 'Pacific', the unique 'W1' 4-6-4 No. 10000 (BR No. 60700) was a rebuild of the experimental high-pressure four-cylinder compound which featured a water-tube boiler and emerged from Darlington Works in 1929. This brave and futuristic design suffered from heavy coal consumption and other serious problems, and towards the end of 1936 it was sent to Doncaster for rebuilding as a straightforward three-cylinder 4-6-4. It emerged with 'A4'-type streamlining and became a thoroughly useful locomotive on heavy passenger trains, often between London King's Cross and Leeds.

'K4' 2-6-0

Shortly after its restoration in 1989, 'K4' 2-6-0 No. 3442 'The Great Marquess' makes a fine sight at the Severn Valley Railway.
Peter Kelly

Railway of origin London & North Eastern Railway
Introduced 1937
Designer Sir Nigel Gresley
Purpose Operations on the West Highland Line
Wheel arrangement 2-6-0
Driving wheel diameter 5 ft 2 in
Cylinders Three (two outside, one inside) 18½ in x 26 in
Tractive effort 36,600 lb
Number built 6

Built specifically for the arduous West Highland Line, the London & North Eastern Railway's six 'K4' 2-6-0s were designed by Sir Nigel Gresley and built at the former North Eastern Railway's Darlington Works in 1937/8. The idea was to have a light yet powerful three-cylinder 2-6-0 with small 5 ft 2 in driving wheels, and they were named 'Loch Long', 'The Great Marquess', 'Cameron of Lochiel', 'Lord of the Isles', 'MacCailinMor' and 'MacLeod of MacLeod'. One of them, No. 3442 (BR No. 61994) 'The Great Marquess', remains in operating condition at the Severn Valley Railway after having a major overhaul completed in 1989. It was restored to main line condition just in time to give its owner, the late Lord Lindsay, the chance to travel with it from Fort William to Mallaig and return before he died.

'Manor' 4-6-0

No. 7828 'Odney Manor' makes crisp work of a passenger train on the East Lancashire Railway in 1990.
Chris Milner

Railway of origin Great Western Railway
Introduced 1938
Designer C.B. Collett
Purpose Wide route availability passenger trains
Wheel arrangement 4-6-0
Driving wheel diameter 5 ft 8 in
Cylinders Two (outside) 18 in x 30 in
Tractive effort 27,340 lb
Number built 30

The rather delicate lines of C.B. Collett's 'Manor' 4-6-0s – built especially for railways such as the Cambrian where heavier locomotives could not operate – can be deceiving, for they proved to be sharp and brisk locomotives with a healthy exhaust 'bark' which on turns such as the 'Cambrian Coast Express' became almost legendary. Introduced in 1938, the 'Manors' were still being produced after the 1948 nationalisation, and eventually numbered thirty examples. As they operated until fairly late in steam days, we are blessed with no fewer than nine preserved examples, including No. 7819 'Hinton Manor' at the Severn Valley Railway, No. 7827 'Lydham Manor' at the Torbay & Dartmouth (South Devon) Railway, and No. 7828 'Odney Manor' at the East Lancashire Railway.

'Queen' 4-6-0

The huge proportions of No. 800 are apparent in this study at Thurles in May 1960.
J.G. Dewing/Colour-Rail

Railway of origin Great Southern Railway, Ireland
Introduced 1939
Designer E.C. Bredin
Purpose Heavy express passenger
Wheel arrangement 4-6-0
Driving wheel diameter 6 ft 7 in
Cylinders Three (two outside, one inside) $18\frac{1}{2}$ in x 28 in
Tractive effort 33,000 lb
Number built Three

These huge and beautiful 4-6-0s were built principally to handle the increasingly heavy passenger trains between Dublin and Cork such as the 'English Mail'. They were named after legendary Irish queens and boasted attractive nameplates in distinctive Erse lettering. The first to appear was No. 800 'Maeve' (later changed to the Irish version 'Maedbh') and its sisters were Nos. 801 'Macha' and 802 'Tailte'. Unfortunately, their introduction coincided with the outbreak of the Second World War (in which Eire remained neutral), so their early activities went largely unrecorded by writers from the British mainland. However, O.S. Nock managed a footplate ride on No. 800 only a few weeks before war was declared and was more than impressed by its performance with a 450-ton load, when it made up time after delays. It proved easily capable of 80 mph running.

'Merchant Navy'

The rebuilt 'Merchant Navy' 'Pacific' No. 35028 'Clan Line' re-enacts a working of the famous 'Golden Arrow' boat train.
Chris Milner

Railway of origin Southern Railway
Introduced 1941
Designer Oliver V.S. Bulleid
Purpose Heavy express passenger
Wheel arrangement 4-6-2
Driving wheel diameter 6 ft 2 in
Cylinders Three (two outside, one inside) 18 in x 24 in
Tractive effort Originally 37,525 lb, reduced to 33,495 lb
Number built 30

Introduced in the depths of wartime, when there was a ban on the construction of purely passenger locomotives, the advanced 'Merchant Navy' 'Pacifics' had to be described as a mixed traffic type. They featured air-smoothed casings, which gave them a boxy look, unusual spokeless wheels and oil-bath-enclosed, chain-driven valve gear. Particularly at home with long and heavy trains on the London-Southampton route, and capable of 100 mph running, the 'Merchant Navies' suffered various mechanical problems in their original guise, and under British Railways ownership were all rebuilt. Their casings were removed, boiler pressure reduced from 280 to 250 lb per sq in, and more conventional valve gear fitted. In their handsome rebuilt form, no fewer than eleven – more than a third of the class – remain in preservation.

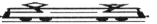

Southern Co-Co Electric

No. 20003 stands under a stormy sky at Eastleigh in May 1959.
The late B.J. Swain/Colour-Rail

Railway of origin Southern Railway
Introduced 1941
Manufacturer SR Ashford
Purpose Mixed traffic
Wheel arrangement Co-Co
Power equipment 630-750 V dc from collector shoe and
overhead equipment, transmission through six English
Electric traction motors, giving 1,470 hp
Tractive effort 40,000 lb max (45,000 lb No. 20003)
Number built 3

Although electric multiple unit trains were the norm
on the Southern Railway's expanding third-rail
system, two Co-Co locomotives, Nos. CC1 and CC2,
were built at Ashford Works during the war for the
haulage of passenger trains and freight over
electrified parts of that railway. As well as being able
to pick up from either collector shoes or pantograph,
these locomotives also had heavy flywheels on their
generator shafts to keep the traction motors
energised at short gaps in the third rail supply.
Although their output was a modest 1,470 hp, Nos
CC1 and CC2 (BR Nos. 20001 and 20002) had a
useful tractive effort of 40,000 lb. In 1948 a third
member of the class, No. 20003, was built.

'USA' 0-6-0 Tank

'USA' tank locomotive No. 30072 at work at Keighley, on the Keighley & Worth Valley Railway.
Chris Milner

Railway of origin US Army Transportation Corps, later Southern Railway
Introduced 1942
Designer Vulcan Works, Wilkes-Barre, PA, USA
Purpose Freight marshalling
Wheel arrangement 0-6-0
Driving wheel diameter 4 ft 6 in
Cylinders Two (outside) 16½ in x 24 in
Tractive effort 21,600 lb
Number built 14

Along with the 'WD' 2-10-0 and 2-8-0 classes built for the Ministry of Supply from 1943 onwards, the 'USA' 0-6-0 tank engines built in the United States for the US Army Transportation Corps were a legacy of the Second World War. They were eventually bought by the Southern Railway in 1946. The fourteen locomotives so purchased, with their two large outside cylinders and easily-reached working parts, were fitted with modified driving cabs and coal bunkers and proved free-steaming and useful shunting locomotives, principally around the Southampton Docks area. Under British Railways, they were numbered from 30061 to 30074, and four of them are still around in preservation; No. 30064 at the Bluebell Railway, Nos. 30065/70 at the Kent & East Sussex Railway and No. 30072 at the Keighley & Worth Valley Railway.

'Q1' 0-6-0

No. 33020 at Nine Elms on 26 June 1960. A 'Lord Nelson' 4-6-0 can be seen in the background.
R.C. Riley

Railway of origin Southern Railway
Introduced 1942
Designer O.V.S. Bulleid
Purpose Freight
Wheel arrangement 0-6-0
Driving wheel diameter 5 ft 1 in
Cylinders Two (inside) 19 in x 26 in
Tractive effort 30,080 lb
Number built 40

Built under wartime conditions and without any regard to niceties such as appearance, Bulleid's 'Austerity' 0-6-0s were designed for cheapness, simplicity and maximum tractive effort for low axle weight (which would allow them to operate widely over the system) in answer to a demand for more goods engines on the Southern Railway. The result was a thoroughly capable locomotive with a high '5F' power classification. To save weight, the 'Q1s' were devoid of wheel splashers and running plates and the simple-sectioned boiler lagging was unusual to say the least. It was not unknown for these 'ugly ducklings' to be pressed into passenger traffic. Of the forty that were built, only one, No. 33001, survives in the National Collection at the Bluebell Railway.

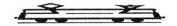

'B1' 4-6-0

No. 1306 'Mayflower' at Swithland Reservoir, Great Central Railway, in 1981.
Chris Milner

Railway of origin London & North Eastern Railway
Introduced 1942
Designer Edward Thompson
Purpose Mixed traffic
Wheel arrangement 4-6-0
Driving wheel diameter 6 ft 2 in
Cylinders Two (outside) 20 in x 26 in
Tractive effort 26,880 lb
Number built 400-plus

Following the sudden death of the London & North Eastern Railway's Chief Mechanical Engineer Sir Herbert Nigel Gresley after a heart attack in 1941, his successor Edward Thompson had to design some simple yet rugged general-purpose locomotives to suit the prevailing wartime conditions, and his two-cylinder 'B1' 4-6-0s were the result. Designed to fulfil much the same role as the LMS 'Black Five' 4-6-0s, the 'B1s' were competent performers and eventually numbered more than 400. With round rather than square-topped fireboxes, they differed visually from their LMS counterparts, and the first forty-one eventually bore the names of varieties of antelope. Footplate crew generally considered them to be good all-rounders, though with riding qualities which varied from acceptable to rough. Preserved are Nos. 1264 (BR No. 61264) and No. 1306 (61306) 'Mayflower'.

'Royal Scot' 4-6-0

No. 6100 'Royal Scot' at the Bressingham Steam Centre, Norfolk, in 1989. The chairs were for a ceremony at which a scheme was announced to raise funds for its rebuilding to full main line condition.
Peter Kelly

Railway of origin London Midland & Scottish Railway
Introduced 1943, as rebuilds of 1927 design
Designer Sir William A. Stanier, from Henry Fowler
Purpose Express passenger
Wheel arrangement 4-6-0
Driving wheel diameter 6 ft 9 in
Cylinders Three (two outside, one inside) 18 in x 26 in
Tractive effort 33,150 lb
Number built 71

Designed originally for the London Midland & Scottish Railway as a parallel boiler design, the 'Royal Scot' 4-6-0s were all rebuilt by William A. Stanier from 1943 (the year of his knighthood) onwards, although in 1935 he had already rebuilt the experimental high-pressure locomotive No. 6399 'Fury' in a fairly similar fashion. With a higher tractive effort than the Great Western 'Castle' 4-6-0s, the 'Scots' were immensely capable locomotives, in charge of a high proportion of important express passenger trains between London Euston and Birmingham, Manchester, Liverpool, Holyhead, Carlisle and Glasgow. They also did sterling work on the Liverpool-Leeds line and other important shorter routes, and it was not uncommon for them to take on the same roles as the London Midland's big 'Pacifics'.

'WD' 2-10-0

'WD' 2-10-0 No. 600 'Gordon' at Bewdley, Severn Valley Railway.
Chris Milner

Railway of origin As specified by War Department
Introduced 1943
Designer Robert A. Riddles
Purpose Heavy freight
Wheel arrangement 2-10-0
Driving wheel diameter 4 ft 8½ in
Cylinders Two (outside) 19 in × 28 in
Tractive effort 34,215 lb
Number built Unspecified: twenty-five bought by BR in 1948

During the 1939-45 World War, many hundreds of locomotives of the 2-8-0 and 2-10-0 freight wheel arrangement, designed by Robert A. Riddles, were built for the Ministry of Supply to a standard 'austerity' War Department specification. Both types, introduced in 1943, were no-nonsense, slogging engines designed for the roughest of service conditions abroad in newly-liberated countries. After the war, British Railways bought large numbers of the 2-8-0 locomotives for its own use: they eventually numbered more than 700 in the 90000 series. In addition, twenty-five of the larger 2-10-0s were purchased, and one of the locomotives to this general design, the Longmoor Military Railway's No. 600 'Gordon', can still be seen at the Severn Valley Railway in its smart blue and red colour scheme. Others are at the Mid-Hants Railway and North Yorkshire Moors Railway.

'County' 4-6-0

A powerful image of a 'County' as No. 1011 'County of Chester' gets away from Didcot with a Stephenson Locomotive Society special in September 1964.
J.P. Aylard/Colour-Rail

Railway of origin Great Western Railway
Introduced 1945
Designer F.W. Hawksworth
Purpose Fast mixed traffic
Wheel arrangement 4-6-0
Driving wheel diameter 6 ft 3 in
Cylinder Two (outside) 18½ in x 30 in
Tractive effort 32,580 lb
Number built 30

The last type of main line express locomotive designed for the Great Western Railway, the 'County' 4-6-0s broke away from the traditional mould in several important ways. A very high boiler pressure of 280 lb per sq in and a boiler based on those of the Stanier '8F' 2-8-0s built at Swindon Works during the war years resulted in an extremely lively locomotive which came between a 'Hall' and 'Castle' 4-6-0 in the power stakes. With a tractive effort of 32,580 lb, the 'Counties' had good hill-climbing abilities, and they were often found on the Wolverhampton-Chester route as well as in the west of England. They were built with straight splashers and nameplates rather than the more traditional curved ones, and were named after counties in England and Wales. At first, the 'Counties' had single chimneys, but these were later changed to extremely squat double ones.

Ivatt Class '2MT' 2-6-2 Tank

Ivatt class '2MT' tank locomotive No. 41241 shunts stock at Keighley, on the Keighley & Worth Valley Railway.
Chris Milner

Railway of origin London Midland & Scottish Railway
Introduced 1946
Designer H.G. Ivatt
Purpose Light mixed traffic
Wheel arrangement 2-6-2T
Driving wheel diameter 5 ft 0 in
Cylinders Two (outside) 16 in x 24 in, later batch 16½ in x 24 in
Tractive effort 17,410 lb, later batch 18,510 lb
Number built 130

Introduced in 1946 to the design of H.G. Ivatt, only the first ten of these modern and free-running tank locomotives were built under the auspices of the London Midland & Scottish Railway, the vast majority being completed under the newly nationalised British Railways up to 1952. Intended for use on light local passenger trains and goods duties, many of the 130-strong class (which were numbered from 41200 onwards by BR) were fitted with vacuum control gear to allow them to be used on push-pull trains. On these, the driver (in the leading coach) would communicate with the fireman (on the locomotive footplate at the back of the train, or even sometimes in the middle of the train) by means of a bell code – and the system actually worked!

'A1' 'Pacific'

Roller bearing-fitted 'A1' 'Pacific' No. 60156 'Great Central' at Wood Green on a northbound express on 13 September 1958.
R.C. Riley

Railway of origin London & North Eastern Railway
Introduced 1945 (prototype) and 1948
Designer Edward Thompson (prototype); remainder Arthur H. Peppercorn
Purpose Express passenger
Wheel arrangement 4-6-2
Driving wheel diameter 6 ft 8 in
Cylinders Three (two outside, one inside) 19 in x 26 in
Tractive effort 37,400 lb
Number built 50

The 'A1s', introduced by A.H. Peppercorn in 1948 were an improvement on Edward Thompson's rather unattractive rebuild of the original Gresley 'Pacific' No. 4470 'Great Northern', which became the one and only 'A1/1' in 1945. With their names mounted on smoke-deflectors (whose purpose was to clear drifting smoke from the cab-front windows), Peppercorn's 'A1s' had different front end arrangements from Gresley's pre-war 'Pacifics', and were not quite the racehorses those had been. Nevertheless, they earned a reputation as tireless 'sloggers' with a 100 mph potential, and shared main line duties of every kind with the 'A3' and 'A4' 'Pacifics'. Although not a single 'A1' was saved, an amazing project has been launched to build one from scratch, and this was raising money fast as this book was being put together.

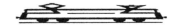

'West Country' 'Pacific'

In its stylish rebuilt form, 'West Country' 'Pacific' No. 34027 'Taw Valley' prepares to leave Crewe with a 'North Wales Coast Express' in 1990.
Chris Milner

Railway of origin Southern Railway
Introduced 1945
Designer O.V.S. Bulleid
Purpose Express passenger
Wheel arrangement 4-6-2
Driving wheel diameter 6 ft 2 in
Cylinders Three (two outside, one inside) $16\frac{3}{8}$ in x 24 in
Tractive effort 27,715 lb
Number built 54

The more numerous of Bulleid's light 'Pacifics', the 'West Countries' carried the names of places in that part of the world once served by the London & South Western Railway, and on whose lines they continued to run wherever their axle loads permitted. On the Waterloo-Exeter route in particular they were capable of some fine performances, and were also used in latter years on the picturesque and rural Somerset & Dorset route, now, sadly, gone for ever. It was not unusual to see a 'West Country' on trains such as the 'Atlantic Coast Express' or prestigious 'Golden Arrow'. A large number are preserved, including the air-smoothed 21C 123 (later BR No. 34023) 'Blackmore Vale' 34092 'City of Wells', and the rebuilt No. 21C 127 (34027) 'Taw Valley'.

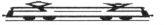

'Battle of Britain' 'Pacific'

The magnificently restored 'Battle of Britain' 'Pacific' No. 34072 '257 Squadron', in its original air-smoothed condition in 1990.
Chris Milner

Railway of origin Southern Railway
Introduced 1946
Designer O.V.S. Bulleid
Purpose Express passenger
Wheel arrangement 4-6-2
Driving wheel diameter 6 ft 2 in
Cylinders Three (two outside, one inside) $16\frac{1}{8}$ in x 24 in
Tractive effort 27,715 lb
Number built 41

Designed as a smaller version of O.V S. Bulleid's 'Merchant Navy' 'Pacifics' of the Southern Railway, the three-cylinder 'Battle of Britain' light 'Pacifics' were built from 1946 until 1951, by which time Britain's railways had been nationalised for more than three years. The 'BBs' embodied many features of their larger counterparts, including a rather neater air-smoothed casing and chain-driven valve gear. Named in honour of the Royal Air Force squadrons, airfields and leaders who had defeated the Luftwaffe during the Second World War, the 'BBs' were often found in Kent. No. 21C 151 (later BR No. 34051) 'Winston Churchill' has been preserved by the National Railway Museum, and other survivors include No. 34072 '257 Squadron' and 21C 167 (34067) 'Tangmere'.

Ivatt Class '2' 2-6-0

Ivatt class '2' 2-6-0 No. 46521 keeps BR Standard class '4' 2-6-4 tank locomotive No. 80079 company at the Severn Valley Railway.
Chris Milner

Railway of origin London Midland & Scottish Railway
Introduced 1946
Designer H.G. Ivatt
Purpose Branch line mixed traffic
Wheel arrangement 2-6-0
Driving wheel diameter 5 ft 0 in
Cylinders Two (outside) 16 in x 24 in, also 16½ in x 24 in
Tractive effort 17,410 lb, also 18,510 lb
Number built 128

The delicate-looking class '2' mixed traffic 2-6-0s
were designed by H.G. Ivatt, the London Midland
& Scottish Railway's Chief Mechanical Engineer
from 1945 until 1947, and that of British Railways'
London Midland Region until 1951. They were
modern, fast and economical and ideally suited to
the light branch line work for which they were
designed. These same qualities make them ideal for
today's preserved railways, and no fewer than seven
are still around at locations ranging from
Steamtown, Carnforth, to the Severn Valley Railway
and Strathspey Railway. The BR Standard class '2'
2-6-0s of the 78000 series were virtually identical
locomotives, and four of these are also preserved.

Ivatt Class '4' 2-6-0

No. 43106 at Bridgnorth, Severn Valley Railway, with an afternoon train to Bewdley on 12 September 1981.
Chris Milner

Railway of origin London Midland & Scottish Railway
Introduced 1947
Designer H.G. Ivatt
Purpose Mixed traffic
Wheel arrangement 2-6-0
Driving wheel diameter 5 ft 3 in
Cylinders Two (outside) 17½ in x 26 in
Tractive effort 24,170 lb
Numbeer built 161

H.G. Ivatt's useful class '4' 2-6-0s or 'Moguls' were designed for the London Midland & Scottish Railway and introduced in 1947, but in fact were mostly built under the newly nationalised British Railways from 1 January 1948 onwards. They reflected the vital need for new general-purpose locomotives which would operate in all conditions with the minimum of maintenance in those grey years which followed the end of the Second World War, which had virtually worn out Britain's railway network. Overall styling was of secondary importance to ease servicing, a trend which was continued with the BR Standard types that followed: the BR class '4' 2-6-0 had identical power characteristics to the Ivatt locomotives but a somewhat tidier look. Many Ivatt class '4s' spent their working lives on other regions such as the Eastern and North Eastern.

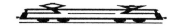

LMS Diesel Electrics

No. 10000 heads the 'Royal Wessex' express near Shawford Junction in 1954.
The late B.J. Swain/Colour-Rail

Railway of origin London Midland & Scottish Railway
Introduced 1947
Manufacturer Derby Works
Purpose Main line mixed traffic
Wheel arrangement Co-Co
Engine Sixteen cylinder English Electric 16SVT diesel producing 1,600 hp
Transmission Electric
Tractive effort 41,400 lb max
Number built 2

The London Midland & Scottish Railway pioneered the use of diesel power in shunting locomotives, but its first main line diesel electrics were the purposeful Co-Cos Nos. 10000 and 10001, the first of which emerged from Derby Works only weeks before nationalisation and so, quite properly, bore the legend 'LMS' on its sides. Although these locomotives were often used singly, on the kind of duties a 'Black Five' steam equivalent might undertake, they eventually became a familiar sight coupled together on important passenger trains such as the 'Royal Scot' on which loadings of fifteen bogies were not uncommon. In 1949, they even completed a London Euston-Glasgow return trip in one day. Both of these pioneering locomotives had been withdrawn by the mid-1960s, and, shamefully, both were broken up.

Gas-Turbine No. 18000

Gas-turbine locomotive No. 18000 stands outside Swindon Works in August 1957.
T.B. Owen/Colour-Rail

Railway of origin British Railways
Introduced 1950
Manufacturer Swiss Locomotive & Machine Works, Winterthur
Purpose Express passenger
Wheel arrangement A1A-A1A
Engine Brown-Boveri gas-turbine producing 2,500 hp
Transmission Electric
Tractive effort 60,000 lb max
Number built 1

One of two gas-turbine locomotives introduced at the beginning of the 1950s to the Western Region of British Railways, No. 18000 was built by the Swiss Locomotive & Machine Works at Winterthur, Switzerland, and quickly gained the nickname of 'Kerosene Castle'. It proved easily capable of handling the often heavy express passenger trains normally entrusted to 'King' or 'Castle' 4-6-0s, and was particularly adept at making up time after late starts, but it has to be said that it also spent a lot of time at Swindon Works! It was often seen on the London Paddington-Bristol route, and underwent numerous trials on the Devon banks moving heavy trains from a standing start. Withdrawn from BR service in 1960 (by which time diesel rather than gas-turbine power had been decided upon) No. 18000 was eventually returned to Switzerland.

Fell Diesel-Mechanical

No. 10100 works a local train near Chapel-en-le-Frith in June 1957.
The late W. Oliver/Colour-Rail

Railway of origin British Railways
Introduced 1951
Designer H.G. Ivatt/Lt-Col L.F.R. Fell
Purpose Experimental
Wheel arrangement 4-8-4
Driving wheel diameter 4 ft 3 in
Engine Four twelve-cylinder Paxman 12 RPH diesel
engines producing a total of 2,000 hp
Transmission Mechanical
Tractive effort 29,400 lb max
Number built 1

This 'ugly duckling', No. 10100, embodied the
highly unusual Fell patent mechanical transmission
through which each of the four twelve-cylinder
Paxman diesel engines was accelerated in turn
through Lt-Col Fell's patent transmission of
differential drive and fluid couplings until, from
about 25 mph to the locomotive's maximum of
about 75 mph, all four engines would be working
hard and producing their maximum 2,000 hp.
Unusually, the engines were housed front and rear,
two each beneath the protruding 'bonnets', with the
transmission machinery in the main body of the
locomotive above the driving wheels. Sadly, the
experiment was concluded after seven years of trials.
When No. 10100 caught fire at Manchester Central
Station in 1958. It never worked again.

Southern Diesel-Electrics

*No. 10203, in immaculate black livery and with silver-painted bogies,
creates a stir with a test train at London Waterloo in April 1954.*
S.C. Townroe/Colour-Rail

Railway of origin British Railways
Introduced 1951
Manufacturer BR Ashford
Purpose Mixed traffic
Wheel arrangement 1 Co-Co 1
Engine Sixteen-cylinder English Electric 16SVT
producing 1,750 hp (No. 10203 16SVT Mk II producing
2,000 hp)
Transmission Electric
Tractive effort 48,000 lb max (50,000 lb No. 10203)
Number built 3

Although their design dates back to the Southern
Railway in the immediate pre-nationalisation years,
it was under the auspices of British Railways that
No. 10201 emerged from Ashford Works in 1951,
followed a year later by its sister locomotive No.
10202. Finally, in 1954, the more powerful No.
10203 made the class a threesome. After undergoing
trials on the Southern Region, all three locomotives
moved to the London Midland, to give a comparison
with the LMS diesel-electrics Nos. 10000 and 10001
on top expresses such as the 'Royal Scot' and
'Mid-Day Scot'. On such duties, Nos. 10201/2
would normally double-head, whereas No. 10203
was more often seen alone.

BR Standard 'Britannia' 'Pacific'

Looking superb after its return to main line steam, No. 70000 'Britannia' prepares to haul the 'Britannia Phoenix' in 1991.
Chris Milner

Railway of origin British Railways
Introduced 1951
Designer BR Derby (built at Crewe)
Purpose Fast mixed traffic
Wheel arrangement 4-6-2
Driving wheel diameter 6 ft 2 in
Cylinders Two (outside) 20 in x 28 in
Tractive effort 32,150 lb
Number built 55

The first large mixed traffic locomotives of the British Railways Standard classes to emerge from Crewe Works, the handsome 'Britannia' 'Pacifics' transformed services between London Liverpool Street, Norwich and other parts of East Anglia from 1951 onwards, and were soon seen on the Southern Region as well, hauling prestige boat trains such as the 'Golden Arrow'. Fast, free-running and always easily capable of exceeding 90 mph on express duties, the 'Britannias' were also straightforward 'sloggers' and eventually found their way on to every region of BR. With their high running plates allowing easier maintenance, these 'Pacifics' set the trend for other Standard designs, and although struck by a number of teething problems, their overall record was excellent.

BR Standard 'Clan' 'Pacific'

BR Standard 'Clan' light 'Pacific' No. 72005 'Clan Macgregor' is coaled up at Perth in June 1962.
H.D. Ramsey/Colour-Rail

Railway of origin British Railways
Introduced 1952
Designer BR Derby (built at Crewe)
Purpose Fast mixed traffic
Wheel arrangement 4-6-2
Driving wheel diameter 6 ft 2 in
Cylinders Two (outside) 19½ in x 28 in
Tractive effort 27,520 lb
Number built 10

A smaller version of the 'Britannia' Standard 'Pacifics', the lighter 'Clans' were consructed for the Scottish Region, where they proved useful on Stranraer boat trains from Carlisle and Glasgow and a variety of other duties including fitted freights and passenger trains which occasionally brought them south of Carlisle. Their power category put them in approximately the same class as the former LMS 'Jubilee' 4-6-0s, and it is generally believed that footplate crews sometimes expected too much of them because they shared the same 'Pacific' chassis as the more powerful 'Britannias'. All ten locomotives were named after Scottish clans, and with smaller boilers and taller chimneys than the 'Britannias', they were certainly handsome-looking engines.

BR Standard Class '5' 4-6-0

At the end of its BR working days, No. 73040 stands forlornly at Bolton Depot, Lancashire, on 17 May 1968.
Eric Sawford

Railway of origin British Railways
Introduced 1951
Designer BR Doncaster, under supervision of R.A. Riddles
Purpose Mixed traffic
Wheel arrangement 4-6-0
Driving wheel diameter 6 ft 2 in
Cylinders Two (outside) 19 in x 28 in
Tractive effort 26,120 lb
Number built 172

Among the first of the British Railways Standard steam designs to emerge in 1951, these popular and reliable mixed traffic locomotives were blessed with particularly free-steaming boilers, and carried out much the same duties as the LMS 'Black Fives', eventually working on every region of BR. Slightly longer-legged than the Stanier locomotives, with driving wheels 2 in larger in diameter, the 73000 series bore all the usual trademarks of the Standards, such as an extremely high running plate exposing mechanical parts for easy maintenance. This gave the handsome locomotives a distinctive frontal wedge beneath the smokebox doors, which made approaching members of the class immediately recognisable.

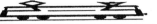

BR Standard Class '4' 4-6-0

As it gleams alongside other locomotives at the Keighley & Worth Valley Railway, it's hard to believe that No. 75078 stood rusting at a scrapyard for five years and seven months.
Chris Milner

Railway of origin British Railways
Introduced 1951
Designer Brighton Drawing Office, under supervision of Robert A. Riddles
Purpose Mixed traffic
Wheel arrangement 4-6-0
Driving wheel diameter 5 ft 8 in
Cylinders Two (outside) 18 in x 28 in
Tractive effort 25,100 lb
Number built 80

Built for reliability and simplicity, with a high route availability, the eighty locomotives of the 75000 series of British Railways Standard steam designs were all constructed at the former Great Western Railway locomotive works at Swindon. They were at home on a variety of duties, and some acquired double chimneys during their working lives. The example shown, No. 75078, built at the beginning of 1956, was withdrawn only ten years later. It went to Dai Woodham's scrapyard at Barry, South Wales, where it stood rusting yet escaping the cutter's torch until 1972. After being rescued, it was restored at Haworth, on the Keighley & Worth Valley Railway, where it can still be seen today.

BR Standard Class '4' 2-6-4 Tank

No. 80080 was in immaculate condition when pictured on this 'Derwent Explorer' steam special.
Chris Milner

Railway of origin British Railways
Introduced 1951
Designer Brighton Drawing Office under supervision of Robert A. Riddles
Purpose Short-distance mixed traffic
Wheel arrangement 2-6-4
Driving wheel diameter 5 ft 8 in
Cylinders Two (outside) 18 in x 28 in
Tractive effort 25,100 lb
Number built 155

One of twelve designs of British Railways Standard locomotives built under the direction of Robert A. Riddles from 1951 onwards, the mixed traffic class '4' 2-6-4 tank locomotives in the 80000 series were designed at Brighton and had more than a passing resemblance to similar locomotive types built for the London Midland & Scottish Railway. The Standard design, though, was perhaps the most handsome of them all, and with their two big outside cylinders and good adhesion qualities (as the weight of the side water tanks was over the 5 ft 8 in driving wheels) the locomotives proved to be powerful and versatile. They gave useful service in many parts of the country until their short-lived reign was cut short by the demise of steam in Britain.

Gas Turbine No. 18100

Brand new, the Metropolitan-Vickers gas turbine No. 18100 poses for its official portrait outside the works in 1952.
Colin Marsden/Colour-Rail

Railway of origin British Railways
Introduced 1952
Manufacturer Metropolitan-Vickers Electrical Co Ltd
Purpose Express passenger
Wheel arrangement Co-Co
Engine Gas turbine producing 3,000 hp
Transmission Electric
Tractive effort 60,000 lb max
Number built 1

Metropolitan-Vickers' entry into the gas turbine field arrived a little later than the Brown-Boveri locomotive, No. 18000 being completed at the end of 1952 and entering service on the Western Region at the start of the following year. With a 3,000 hp rating, it was slightly more powerful than the Swiss version, and was tried out on various express turns such as the 'Merchant Venturer' from London Paddington to Bristol. Like No. 18000, though, No. 18100 spent long periods out of use and in 1958 Metropolitan-Vickers rebuilt it as a straight 25 kV ac electric locomotive with four traction motors instead of the previous six, making it an A1A-A1A rather than a Co-Co. In this form it was renumbered E2001 and used for the training of drivers for the London Midland Region's electrification between Crewe, Manchester and Liverpool. After four years out of service, it was broken up in the early 1970s.

BR Standard Class '4' 2-6-0

A grubby No. 76051 sets off from Harston Sidings on 4 June 1966.
Eric Sawford

Railway of origin British Railways
Introduced 1953
Designer BR Doncaster, under supervision of R. A. Riddles
Purpose Mixed traffic
Wheel arrangement 4-6-0
Driving wheel diameter 5 ft 3 in
Cylinders Two (outside) 17½ in x 26 in
Tractive effort 24,170 lb
Number built 115

Developed from the unfortunately nicknamed (although always strong and reliable) 'Black Pig' 2-6-0s which were designed by H.G. Ivatt for the London Midland & Scottish Railway and introduced in 1947, the BR Standard class '4' 2-6-0s which emerged five years later had exactly the same driving wheel diameter, cylinder dimensions and tractive effort as their LMS counterparts. The combination of small driving wheels and high running plates gave the LMS version a businesslike but untidy appearance, but the BR Standard version looked much tidier especially around the front end. The 115 members of the 76000 series put in some sound medium mixed traffic work over a wide area of BR, although unfortunately they had relatively short lives.

BR Standard Class '2' 2-6-0

No. 78028 handles a ballast train at Groby in May 1964.
R.C. Riley

Railway of origin British Railways
Introduced 1953
Designer BR Derby under supervision of R.A. Riddles
Purpose Light mixed traffic
Wheel arrangement 2-6-0
Driving wheel diameter 5 ft 0 in
Cylinders Two (outside) 16½ in x 24 in
Tractive effort 18,515, lb
Number built 65

Almost identical to the class '2' 2-6-0s designed by H.G. Ivatt for the London Midland & Scottish Railway in 1946, the sixty-five locomotives in the 78000 series enjoyed the economy and free-running characteristics of a thoroughly modern design, and proved highly useful on light pick-up and branch duties of all descriptions. With an extremely low axle loading, their range was widely spread and they could be found on all regions except the Southern. No fewer than four have been rescued from Barry Scrapyard – Nos. 78018, 78019, 78022 and 78059 – the latter having stood there derelict for over fifteen years. No. 78018 is being restored at Darlington, and others can be found at the Severn Valley Railway, Bluebell Railway and Keighley & Worth Valley Railway.

Class '08' Shunter

Grey-livered class '08' No. 08 924 was pictured at Birmingham New Street on 16 August 1991.
Geoff Kelly

Railway of origin British Railways
Introduced 1953
Manufacturer BR at various loco works
Purpose General shunting and pilot duties
Wheel arrangement 0-6-0
Engine English Electric six-cylinder 6KT giving 400 hp
Transmission Electric
Tractive effort 35,000 lb max
Number built 1,000 plus

Outside nearly every major station in Britain and in goods sidings the length and breadth of the country, the class '08' 0-6-0 diesel electric shunters can be seen at work or awaiting their next duties. Their pedigree goes right back to London Midland & Scottish Railway days in the mid-1930s, when diesel power was first being considered to replace steam on station pilot and marshalling yard duties. Built from 1953 onwards at locations as widespread as Crewe, Darlington, Derby, Doncaster and Horwich, well over 1,000 examples were eventually at work. With changing practices on today's railway, though, many duties such as the marshalling of carriages have declined, and in recent years the ranks of class '08s' have thinned considerably. Many of the locomotives have been painted in individual local colour schemes, but most are in blue or grey.

BR Standard Class '8' 'Pacific'

The majestic class '8' 'Pacific' No. 71000 'Duke of Gloucester' looks as good as new as it heads a steam special. It's hard to believe it stood in Barry scrapyard for six and a half years!
Chris Milner

Railway of origin British Railways
Introduced 1954
Designer BR Derby (built at Crewe)
Purpose Heavy express passenger
Wheel arrangement 4-6-2
Driving wheel diameter 6 ft 2 in
Cylinders Three (two outside, one inside) 18 in x 28 in
Tractive effort 39,080 lb
Number built 1

Built as a replacement for the 'Princess Royal' 'Pacific' No. 46202 'Princess Anne', which was itself rebuilt from the Stanier-designed 'Turbomotive' and unfortunately destroyed in the Harrow disaster of 1952, No. 71000 'Duke of Gloucester' was unique being the only BR Standard to feature three cylinders. Other interesting features were its rotary Caprotti valve gear and its double chimney. Withdrawn in 1962 after only eight years' service, it was stored for a while pending preservation, but only one cylinder and its associated valve gear were required, and it was dumped in Barry scrapyard in October 1967. Miraculously, it has now been completely rebuilt and is a star main line performer once more.

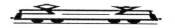

BR Standard Class '9F' 2-10-0

BR Standard '9F' 2-10-0 No. 92220 'Evening Star' passes Sutton Bridge Junction, Shrewsbury, with a 'Welsh Marches Pullman'.
Chris Milner

Railway of origin British Railways
Introduced 1954
Designer Robert A. Riddles
Purpose Heavy freight
Wheel arrangement 2-10-0
Driving wheel diameter 5 ft 0 in
Cylinders Two (outside) 20 in x 28 in
Tractive effort 39,670 lb
Number built 251

The sole freight-only design introduced in the range of British Railways Standard steam locomotives under Robert A. Riddles was the handsome, modern and immensely capable '9F' 2-10-0. The last Standard '9F' was No. 92220, built at Swindon, and as this was BR's final steam locomotive, it was specially turned out in dark green, fitted with many Great Western-style embellishments and named 'Evening Star'. No. 92220 is now in the National Collection, and has been a regular main line performer on steam specials. Others preserved include No. 92203 'Black Prince' at the East Somerset Railway.

'Deltic' Prototype

The startling blue and cream colour scheme of the 'Deltic' prototype is seen to good effect as it heads for London King's Cross in June 1959.
P.J. Hughes/Colour-Rail

Railway of origin Private venture on British Railways
Introduced 1955
Manufacturer English Electric Co
Purpose Experimental high-speed express passenger
Wheel arrangement Co-Co
Engine Two eighteen-piston Napier 'Deltic' two-stroke diesel engines producing a total of 3,300 hp
Transmission Electric
Tractive effort 60,000 lb max
Number built 1

When the prototype 'Deltic' was first seen – and heard – on the steam-dominated British Railways in 1955, its effect was startling. Finished in bright blue, with cream-coloured chevrons on its streamlined nose-ends, it was immediately recognisable and had the awesome reputation of being the most powerful single-unit diesel locomotive in the world. Easily a match for the main line 'Pacifics' of the day, it coped with heavy trains such as the London Euston-Liverpool 'Red Rose' with ease, and was later transferred to the Eastern Region on which it demonstrated the shape of things to come between London King's Cross and Leeds. The twenty-two production 'Deltics' (later class '55') which followed in 1961 became the backbone of East Coast main line services until they were replaced by Intercity 125 trains.

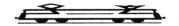

Class '20'

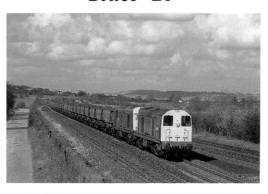

Class 20s Nos. 20 007/157 head a coal train at Shipley Gate on 17 March 1991.
Colin J. Marsden

Railway of origin British Railways
Introduced 1957
Manufacturer English Electric, Vulcan Foundry
Purpose Light mixed traffic, particularly freight
Wheel arrangement Bo-Bo
Engine Eight-cylinder English Electric 8SVT Mk II producing 1,000 hp
Transmission Electric
Tractive effort 42,000 lb max
Number built 228

One of the longest-lived of diesel electric classes on British Railways today, the English Electric Type 1 (later class '20') Bo-Bos were introduced as long ago as 1957, when a pilot batch of twenty (Nos. D8000-8019) was built at Vulcan Foundry, Newton-le-Willows. Further orders were placed until by 1968 no fewer than 228 had been constructed, some at Robert Stephenson & Hawthorn's, Darlington. The first locos went to Bow, North London, where they worked on local freight duties, but numbers eventually spread over a wide area, taking in London Midland, Scottish and Eastern Regions. At their most useful coupled bonnet to bonnet, so that the driver's view is not hindered by the long 'nose', they have been deployed on many different duties from 'merry-go-round' coal to summer holiday specials – and even Channel Tunnel work.

Class '31'

Unusually painted in InterCity colours, No. 31 423 stands at Saltley Depot.
Chris Milner

Railway of origin British Railways
Introduced 1957
Manufacturer Brush Traction, Loughborough
Purpose Mixed traffic
Wheel arrangement A1A-A1A
Engine Twelve-cylinder English Electric 12SVT
producing 1,470 hp
Transmission Electric
Tractive effort 42,000 lb
Number built 260 plus

Among the longest-serving diesel electric locomotives
on British Railways, originally known as the Brush
Type '2s' and numbered in the D5500 series, the
class '31' A1A-A1As were introduced as long ago as
1957 when the first example emerged from Brush.
Originally based on the Eastern Region, their sphere
of operation spread quite widely over the years, and
although their numbers are now dwindling, a
number remain at work on a variety of duties, and
they have more than earned their keep on both
freight and passenger trains with a medium power
requirement. Originally fitted with power units
from Mirrlees, Bickerton & Day which proved
disappointing, all were eventually re-engined with
the downrated and therefore reliable English
Electric engines which remain 'on board' today.
These drive through only four traction motors.

Class '24'

No. 24 025 and another locomotive from the same class pictured in 1977, by which time their ranks were already considerably reduced.
Colin J. Marsden

Railway of origin British Railways
Introduced 1958
Manufacturer BR at Derby, Crewe and Darlington
Purpose Medium mixed traffic
Wheel arrangement Bo-Bo
Engine Six-cylinder Sulzer 6LDA28 diesel producing 1,160 hp
Transmission Electric
Tractive effort 40,000 lb max
Number built 140-plus

More than 450 of the Type 2 Bo-Bo mixed traffic diesel electrics of classes '24/1', '24/2' and '25' were built for British Railways from 1958 onwards, and their duties were roughly similar to those of class '4' or '5' steam locomotives. With widespread changes from locomotive-hauled to diesel and electric multiple unit stock over the years, and loss of the once common short goods train in favour of heavier and more specialised freight operations, the reasons for these locomotives' existence simply trickled away over the years, until today none is left in main line service. The last survivor, formerly No. 25 912 'Tamworth Castle', now preserved, was retained as a training locomotive and in its original green paintwork ran several railtours until 1991.

Class '26'

No. 26 005 in the Railfreight colour scheme of its latter years. The black diamonds indicate it was working for the coal sub-sector.
Chris Milner

Railway of origin British Railways
Introduced 1958
Manufacturer Birmingham Railway Carriage & Wagon Co
Purpose Light mixed traffic
Wheel arrangement Bo-Bo
Engine Six-cylinder Sulzer 6LDA28 producing 1,160 hp
Transmission Electric
Tractive effort 42,000 lb max
Number built 47

From the late 1950s, right through the next two decades and well into the 1980s, the Smethwick-built BRC&W Ltd Type 2 Bo-Bo diesel electrics, later to become classes '26' and '27' (depending on the type of traction motor used) were synonymous with the cities and wide open spaces of Scotland, even though many had started their lives working out of London's King's Cross and St Pancras stations. They became the prime motive power, often double-headed, on romantic lines such as the West Highland from Glasgow Queen Street to Fort William and Mallaig, the Highland main line from Perth to Inverness, and the lines from there to Kyle of Lochalsh, Wick and Thurso. Even today, long after their reign has ended, it is impossible to imagine Kyle without the rattle of their simple yet rugged six-cylinder Sulzer engines turning over.

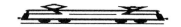

North British 'Warship'

No. D600 'Active' was almost new when this photograph was taken.
R.C. Riley

Railway of origin British Railways
Introduced 1958
Manufacturer North British Locomotive Co
Purpose Express passenger
Wheel arrangement A1A-A1A
Engine Two twelve-cylinder MAN L12V18/21A diesel
engines each producing 1,000 hp
Transmission Hydraulic
Tractive effort 49,460 lb max
Number built 5

The pioneering five 'Warship' diesel-hydraulics
built for BR's Western Region by the North British
Locomotive Co suffered from too much weight at
117 tons and had an A1A-A1A wheel arrangement
which did not allow them the best traction
performance. Apart from this, Nos. D600 'Active',
D601 'Ark Royal', D602 'Bulldog', D603
'Conquest' and D604 'Cossack' were highly
complicated machines introduced at a time when
steam technology still handled the bulk of Britain's
railway traffic, so they never enjoyed the best
servicing environment. Even the D800 series
'Warships' which succeeded them did not enjoy
long working lives although they came a little closer
to the standards set by the German V200s on which
they were based.

'Warship'

No. D821 'Greyhound', beautifully restored to its BR blue livery, on the wheel lathe at Laira Depot, Plymouth, in the autumn of 1991.
Colin J. Marsden

Railway of origin British Railways
Introduced 1958
Manufacturer BR Swindon
Purpose Express passenger
Wheel arrangement B-B
Engine Two twelve-cylinder Bristol Siddeley-Maybach diesel engines producing a total of 2,200 hp and driving through two Mekydro hydraulic transmissions
Transmission Hydraulic
Tractive effort 52,400 lb max
Number built 38

Although five A1A-A1A 'Warship' diesel hydraulic locomotives were built by the North British Locomotive Co for the Western Region of British Railways in 1953, for the main production series it was decided to follow closely the more compact design of the already successful V200 B-B locomotives already at work on the German Federal Railway. The V200's builders, Krauss-Maffei, helped BR to suit the outer design to the British loading gauge, and the powerful class '42' Warships' were the result. Between 1958 and 1961 thirty-eight were built, and all apart from one, No. D812 'The Royal Naval Reserve, 1859–1959' were named after warships. Three remain in preservation – No. D818 'Glory', No. D821 'Greyhound', and No. D832 'Onslaught'.

English Electric Type 4

The first EE Type 4, No. D200, stands alongside Brush Type 2 (later class '31' No. D5583 at Stratford Works on 26 March 1991.
Colin J. Marsden

Railway of origin British Railways
Introduced 1958
Manufacturer English Electric, Vulcan Foundry and Robert Stephenson & Hawthorn
Purpose Mixed traffic, primarily passenger
Wheel arrangement 1 Co-Co 1
Engine Sixteen-cylinder English Electric 16SVT Mk II producing 2,000 hp
Transmission Electric
Tractive effort 52,000 lb max
Number built 200

The English Electric Type 4s, or 'Whistlers' as they became known, first hit the headlines when No. D200, carrying a large headboard proclaiming 'First 2,000 hp Diesel London – Norwich' left London Liverpool Street to mark the new age in 1958. They were gradually introduced to some other regions, primarily the London Midland, and were soon heading many famous expresses. As most carriages at that time were steam-heated, the locomotives had a boiler on board and could replenish their water supplies from troughs which then still stood between the lines in many places. In their later years, they handled mostly freight traffic.

Metrovick Co-Bo

Towards the end of its brief existence, Metrovick Co-Bo No. D5715 stands at Crewe Works on 12 June 1967.
Eric Sawford

Railway of origin British Railways
Introduced 1958
Manufacturer Metropolitan Vickers
Purpose Mixed traffic
Wheel arrangement Co-Bo
Engine Eight-cylinder Crossley HST V8 two-stroke diesel producing 1,200 hp
Transmission Electric
Tractive effort 50,000 lb max
Number built 20

Made famous in a dramatic painting by the great railway artist Terence Cuneo, depicting the 'Condor' (container door-to-door) fast fitted freight train, the twenty Metropolitan Vickers Type 2 diesel electric Co-Bos led fairly unhappy lives. Introduced in 1958 and numbered D5700-D5719, they were first based at Derby and Cricklewood, but soon encountered mechanical problems which took them out of service and into store one by one while their fate was decided. At one time, only two of them were still at work! The locomotives were eventually returned to their manufacturer for corrective treatment, and from 1962 until the end of their short and miserable lives in 1968 they worked from Barrow and Workington over the London Midland Region's Furness and West Cumberland areas on both passenger and freight duties. One survives.

'Baby Deltic'

'Baby Deltic' No. D5905 passes New Southgate with a local suburban service out of London King's Cross in June, 1963.
H.D. Ramsey/Colour-Rail

Railway of origin British Railways
Introduced 1959
Manufacturer English Electric Co, Vulcan Foundry, Newton-le-Willows
Purpose Suburban passenger
Wheel arrangement Bo-Bo
Engine Nine-cylinder, eighteen-piston Napier 'Deltic' two-stroke diesel producing 1,100 hp
Transmission Electric
Tractive effort 46,200 lb max
Number built 10

Definitely the black sheep of the English Electric family, the 'Baby Deltics', which later became known as class '23s' had more than their fair share of engine problems, and from the delivery of the first examples in 1959 to the withdrawal of the last of the class in 1971, their entire spread of service lasted less than twelve years. The 'Baby Deltics', numbered from D5900 to D5909, were to be found on suburban services out of King's Cross, but spent long periods of their lives back at the works receiving attention and, eventually, complete refurbishment. In the end, though, such a small class – only ten locomotives were ever built – simply wasn't economical to operate, and all were withdrawn.

Class '33'

An immaculate class '33', No. 33 034 'Spitfire' gleams at Eastleigh after its naming ceremony in 1991.
Chris Milner

Railway of origin British Railways
Introduced 1959
Manufacturer Birmingham Railway Carriage & Wagon Co
Purpose Mixed traffic
Wheel arrangement Bo-Bo
Engine Eight-cylinder Sulzer 8LDA28 giving 1,550 hp
Transmission Electric
Tractive effort 45,000 lb max
Number built 98

The Southern Region's own straightforward diesel electrics, as opposed to electro-diesels which can pick up current from the 'third rail' system, are the BRCW Type 3s which were later classified '33'. They can still be seen on a variety of duties, now mainly freight, in the south of England. Outwardly almost identical to the BRCW Type 2 Bo-Bos, which became classes '26' and '27', the class '33s' have a more powerful eight-cylinder engine, and different cab ends and suspension details. As they were designed specifically for the Southern Region, they were built with electric heating apparatus, and some were modified for push-pull operations, their drivers being able actually to control the motors of any electric multiple unit that might be included in the train formation. A dozen of these locos were built with narrower bodies.

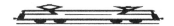

'Blue Pullman'

One of the 'Blue Pullman' power cars at Old Oak Common on 10 September 1960.
R.C. Riley

Railway of origin British Railways
Introduced 1959
Manufacturer Metropolitan-Cammell
Purpose Express passenger
Wheel arrangement Leading bogies of power cars not motored, trailing bogies motored along with leading bogies of first carriage
Engine One twelve-cylinder MAN L12V18/21BS vee-configuration diesel engine producing 1,000 hp in each power car
Transmission Electric
Tractive effort N/A
Number built 5 sets (10 power cars)

The 'Blue Pullman' diesel electric trains were a bold step into the future when they were introduced on the 'Midland Pullman' service between Manchester Central and London St Pancras in 1960. Although built in 1959, the trains were late entering service because of dining car staff disputes, and surprisingly the 'Blue Pullman' riding qualities also left a lot to be desired. They were introduced to the Western Region on 'Bristol Pullman' and 'Birmingham Pullman' trains, and finally came a 'South Wales Pullman' service. It was not easy to utilise the trains to their best advantage though, and they stood idle between workings for long periods. Eventually, they were all withdrawn in 1973.

Class '37'

No. 37 350, specially painted in original green, and No. 37 220, in Railfreight's petroleum livery, await their next duty. A third class '37' in blue can just be seen in the background.
Chris Milner

Railway of origin British Railways
Introduced 1960
Manufacturer English Electric Co, Vulcan Foundry, Newton-le-Willows and Robert Stephenson & Hawthorn, Darlington
Purpose Mixed traffic
Wheel arrangement Co-Co
Engine Twelve-cylinder English Electric 12CSVT producing 1,750 hp
Transmission Electric
Tractive effort 55,500 lb max
Number built 300-plus

One of the most successful designs of diesel electric to come from the English Electric Co, and built both at Vulcan Foundry and Darlington, the Type 3 (later class '37') Co-Cos have proved rugged, versatile and reliable machines. With a more advanced wheel arrangement than the class '40s' that preceded them, they have been equally at home on passenger or freight duties, although in recent years they have been almost entirely confined to freight. Their throaty roar is easily recognisable, as they power freight trains through town and countryside, mostly at night and often working in multiple.

Gas Turbine No. GT3

In this extremely rare colour picture, GT3 is seen at Wendover in September 1961.
J.P. Mullett/Colour-Rail

Railway of origin Private venture on British Railways
Introduced 1961
Manufacturer English Electric Co, Vulcan Foundry, Newton-le-Willows
Purpose Experimental
Wheel arrangement 4-6-0
Engine Gas turbine producing 2,750 hp
Transmission Mechanical
Tractive effort 60,000 lb max
Number built 1

The final attempt at producing a worthwhile gas turbine locomotive in Britain resulted in English Electric's strikingly beautiful GT3, which had the look of a streamlined 4-6-0 steam locomotive and was finished in an unusual light chestnut colour which suited its shape extremely well. Unlike gas turbines Nos. 18000 and 18100, GT3 utilised a mechanical transmission, its turbine engine being coupled to a gearbox on the central driving axle. The load was spread to the outer driving axles by coupling rods, steam locomotive-style. Although GT3 performed well in trials on the London Midland Region, some problems were encountered with the flexible-drive transmission and the experiment was brought to a close. The 'tender' behind GT3's driving cab carried fuel and a train heating boiler.

'Deltic'

*'Deltics' were never noted for clean exhausts, as this picture of the
immaculately restored No. D9000 'Royal Scots Grey' shows.*
Chris Milner

Railway of origin British Railways
Introduced 1961
Manufacturer English Electric
Purpose High-speed express passenger
Wheel arrangement Co-Co
Engine Two eighteen-piston opposed-piston Napier
'Deltic' two-stroke diesel engines producing a total of
3,300 bhp
Transmission Electric
Tractive effort 50,000 lb
Number built 22

Few modern locomotive types have equalled the
impact made by the ultra-powerful 'Deltic' diesel
electrics. They were the mainstay of express services
on the King's Cross to Edinburgh main line from
their introduction in 1961 until they were replaced
by the 125 mph Intercity 125 trains in the late 1970s.
Only twenty-two in number, they displaced a large
number of steam locomotives and were worked
intensively on services to Leeds, Hull, Doncaster,
York, Newcastle-upon-Tyne, Edinburgh and
Aberdeen, being required to run flat out at 100 mph
for much of the time. Named after a mixture of
regiments and racehorses, they had the distinctive
exhaust note which only thirty-six two-stroke
pistons working in harmony could produce!

Class '46'

No. 46 036 passes Dawlish, Devon, with a heavy passenger train in 1977.
Colin J. Marsden

Railway of origin British Railways
Introduced 1961
Manufacturer BR
Purpose Express passenger and mixed traffic
Wheel arrangement 1 Co-Co 1
Engine Twelve-cylinder Sulzer 12LDA28-B twin-bank, pressure-charged diesel producing 2,500 hp
Transmission Electric
Tractive effort 70,000 lb max
Number built 56

The class '46' was the final version of the massively built, Sulzer-powered 1 Co-Co 1 diesel electrics commonly known as 'Peaks' because the first ten (class '44') were named after mountains. Two of these, Nos. D4 (later 44 004) 'Great Gable' and D8 (44 008) 'Penyghent' survive in preservation. About another 180 were built and, according to detail differences such as the type of traction motor used, classified '45' or '46'. During their reign on the London Midland Region these locomotives did some superb work with heavy express trains on the Midland main line between London St Pancras, the Midlands and Manchester, as well as in many other parts of the country. They were just as likely to be found on the Western and North Eastern Regions, and in their latter years their prodigious 70,000 lb of tractive effort suited them to heavy freight trains.

'Western' Diesel Hydraulic

D1009 'Western Invader' stands at Plymouth with a train from London Paddington in 1976.
Colin J. Marsden

Railway of origin British Railways
Introduced 1961
Manufacturer BR
Purpose Express passenger
Wheel arrangement C-C
Engine Two twelve-cylinder, V-configuration Maybach MD655 diesel engines producing a total of 2,700 hp.
Transmission Hydraulic
Tractive effort 72,600 lb max
Number built 74

When the Western Region of British Railways made its modernisation plans for the post-steam era, it plumped, uniquely, for diesel-hydraulic rather than diesel-electric power for its main line services, and the fine-looking 'Western' C-Cs, or class '52s' as they later became known, became the top motive power on expresses out of London's Paddington Station. They carried on the Great Western Railway tradition of cast number plates and nameplates, and all had a 'Western' forename, ie 'Western Firebrand', 'Western Warrior', 'Western Glory' and so on. With their two powerful multi-cylinder engines, the 'Westerns' were able to put down a maximum tractive effort of more than 72,000 lb.

'Hymek'

'Hymek' No. D7001 in rail blue (originally they were green with white window surrounds) on goods duty at Kensington Olympia on 6 October 1971.
R.C. Riley

Railway of origin British Railways
Introduced 1961
Manufacturer Beyer Peacock
Purpose Mixed traffic
Wheel arrangement B-B
Engine Sixteen cylinder Bristol-Siddeley/Maybach MD870 diesel producing 1,740 hp
Transmission Hydraulic
Tractive effort 49,700 lb max
Number built 101

The most numerous of the Western Region's short-lived diesel-hydraulic designs, the 'Hymek' B-B locomotives spanned only fourteen years from the time the first example was built in 1961 until the final withdrawal took place in the mid-1970s. Numbered from D7000 to D7100, they had a distinctive appearance with inward-sloping cab ends, and worked all kinds of Western Region traffic, often double-headed. Their single sixteen-cylinder engines (the double units in 'Western' and 'Warship' locomotives had twelve-cylinders each) producing 1,740 hp worked through Stone-Maybach 'Mekydro' hydraulic transmission. No fewer than four of these lively, good-sounding and undeniably good-looking locomotives have been preserved.

Class '85'

No. 85 023 heads the 10.00 London Euston–Stranraer on 16 May, 1987.
Chris Milner

Railway of origin British Railways
Introduced 1961
Manufacturer BR Doncaster Works
Purpose Mixed traffic, mainly express passenger
Wheel arrangement Bo-Bo
Power equipment 25kV ac from overhead equipment.
Transmission through four AEI 189 traction motors,
giving 3,200 hp
Tractive effort 50,000 lb max
Number built 40

Introduced in 1961 as class 'AL5' and originally
numbered E3056-95, the 100 mph class 85 Bo-Bo
electrics, all built at Doncaster Works, were among
the unsung heroes of the London Euston-Glasgow
West Coast Main Line. Never named, like so many
of the class '86s' which followed in 1965, or class
'87s' which came on stream in the 1970s, they just
got on with the job for three decades, pushed more
on to parcels traffic and secondary duties as they
grew older, and built up phenomenal operating
mileages. Their numbers began to dwindle towards
the end of the 1980s as traction motor and other
problems set in, and the last one was withdrawn in
1991.

Brush Type 4 (Class '47')

With its dazzling new paintwork, No. 47 569 had just been named 'The Gloucestershire Regiment' when this picture was taken.
Chris Milner

Railway of origin British Railways
Introduced 1962
Manufacturer Brush Traction and BR Crewe Works
Purpose Main line mixed traffic
Wheel arrangement Co-Co
Engine Sulzer twelve-cylinder twin-bank, pressure-charged diesel producing 2,750 bhp
Transmission Electric
Tractive effort 55,000 - 62,000 lb
Number built 500-plus

For almost three decades the versatile Brush Type 4 Co-Co diesel-electrics (now class '47'), have been the 'jack of all trades' on British Railways, tackling any duty from express passenger to heavy freight traffic. Sadly, scrapping has already made big inroads into their numbers. Originally painted in two-tone green they later took on the drab BR blue livery, but have since emerged in many other paint schemes, the latest being parcels sector red and grey which almost looks as good as their original green! Class '47' locomotives are seen all over the BR network, and are as likely to turn up in Cornwall as Inverness. Many carry nameplates, and they are divided into a number of sub-classes reflecting their individual duties and specifications.

Class '17'

*The solitary preserved 'Clayton' No. D8568, on show at Old Oak
Common Depot on 18 August 1991.*
R.C. Riley

Railway of origin British Railways
Introduced 1962
Manufacturer Clayton Equipment Co and Beyer Peacock
Purpose Shunting and pick-up freight
Wheel arrangement Bo-Bo
Engine Two six-cylinder Paxman 6ZHXL diesel engines
each producing 450 hp, or (experimentally) two eight-
cylinder Rolls-Royce diesel engines each producing 450 hp
Transmission Electric
Tractive effort 40,000 lb max
Number built 117

For such a numerous class, the distinctive 'Clayton'
diesel electrics had a miserably short existence, some
examples only lasting six years or so in BR service, and
none managing to last for a full decade. The unusual
layout, with two long bonnets and a central cab, gave
good all-round visibility compared with other Type 1
designs, especially during shunting operations. Two
batches were built, the first eighty-eight by Clayton,
with GEC electrical equipment, and the remaining
twenty-nine by Beyer Peacock, with Crompton
Parkinson electrical equipment. The locomotives,
numbered from D8500 onwards, did not enjoy good
reliability, and the kind of work for which they were
built declined seriously in the 1960s. Some were sold to
industry, and one of these, No. D8568, has survived in
preservation at the North Yorkshire Moors Railway.

Class '73'

Immaculate after its 'Battle of Britain 50th Anniversary' naming ceremony in the autumn of 1990, No. 73 109 stands at Dover Priory.
Chris Milner

Railway of origin British Railways
Introduced 1962
Manufacturer BR Eastleigh Works and English Electric Co, Vulcan Foundry, Newton-le-Willows, Lancs
Purpose Dual-power mixed traffic
Wheel arrangement Bo-Bo
Power equipment 660-750 V dc from third rail, transmission through four English Electric traction motors, giving 1,600 hp
Engine (for use where non-electrified) English Electric four-cylinder 4SRKT diesel producing 600 hp, transmission electric
Tractive effort 40,000 lb electric; 36,000 lb diesel
Number built 48

Unusual in that they can operate by picking up power from the 660-750V dc third rail system, or under their own diesel power with the four-cylinder English Electric 4SRKT engine fitted, the boxy yet still attractive class '73' Bo-Bo electro-diesels use their versatility to the full on Southern Region Lines, powering 'Gatwick Express' trains from London Waterloo to the airport, and often turned out in gleaming condition to operate the prestigious 'Venice-Simplon Orient Express Pullman' train. The first six were built at Eastleigh Works and the remainder, classified '73/1', emerged from the Vulcan Foundry, Newton-le-Willows.

Experimental 'DP2'

Shortly after being built, 'DP2' stands at Camden Shed, London Midland Region, in plain unlined green in June 1962.
J.G. Dewing/Colour-Rail

Railway of origin British Railways
Introduced 1962
Manufacturer English Electric Co, Vulcan Foundry, Newton-le-Willows
Purpose Experimental express passenger
Wheel arrangement Co-Co
Engine Sixteen-cylinder charge-cooled 16CSVT diesel producing 2,700 hp
Transmission Electric
Tractive effort 50,000 lb max
Number built 1

It looked like a 'Deltic', but it certainly didn't sound like one! 'DP2' (Diesel Prototype 2) used a 'Deltic' body shell to house the latest development of the trusty sixteen-cylinder 16SVT diesel engine, boosted from 1,600 hp in LMS diesel electric No. 10000, then 2,000 hp in the ED Type 4 (later class '40') locomotives, to 2,700 hp through the introduction of charge-air cooling. Pitted against other prototype locomotives such as 'Lion' and 'Falcon', 'DP2' had a lot going for it, not least a decided weight advantage, and it underwent successful trials on the London Midland and Eastern Regions. While heading a King's Cross-Edinburgh express at the end of June 1967, it became involved in a horrific collision which led to the deaths of seven passengers, and was written off.

'Lion' Prototype

'Lion' stands at London Paddington's platform 1 with the 13.35 parcels train for Swindon on 27 June 1962.
Euslin Bruce

Railway of origin Private venture on British Railways
Introduced 1962
Manufacturer Birmingham Railway Carriage & Wagon Co Ltd
Purpose Experimental
Wheel arrangement Co-Co
Engine Uprated Sulzer twelve-cylinder 12LDA, producing 2,750 hp
Transmission Electric
Number built 1

In its startling yet probably quite impractical white livery, the Birmingham Railway Carriage & Wagon Co's 2,750 hp 'Lion' prototype numbered D0260, built at that firm's Smethwick works, utilised a powerful Sulzer twelve-cylinder, twin crankshaft unit from the same family of engines fitted to BR's class, '45', '46' and '47' locomotives, and had a designed maximum speed of 100 mph which was comfortably exceeded during trials. It was formally unveiled on 28 May 1962 at Marylebone Station before undergoing a controlled testing programme on British Railways. Like other powerful prototype locomotives which performed extremely well, it was doomed by the fact that BR was already moving towards the concept of Intercity 125 trains instead of single diesel locomotives on non-electrified major routes.

Class '86'

In Network SouthEast colours, No. 86 401 was a big draw at an open day at Basingstoke in 1987.
Colin J. Marsden

Railway of origin British Railways
Introduced 1965
Manufacturer English Electric Co, Vulcan Foundry, and BR Doncaster
Purpose Express passenger and fast freight
Wheel arrangement Bo-Bo
Power equipment 25 kV ac from overhead equipment, transmission through four GEC frame-mounted traction motors, giving 5,000 hp
Tractive effort 58,000 lb max
Number built 100

For many years the mainstay of express services on the 25 kV ac system of the West Coast Main Line from London Euston to Glasgow, the AL6, later class '86', Bo-Bo electric locomotives were built by the English Electric Co at Vulcan Foundry, Newton-le-Willows, Lancashire, and by BR at Doncaster Works. At first, locomotives in this class were numbered from E 3101 onwards, but upon reclassification they carried the number 86 as a prefix to a new series. Over the years though, these capable 100 mph-plus locomotives have been further modified and sub-classified, and their area of operation has spread with the extension of electrification, principally from London Liverpool Street to Norwich, and now Carstairs to Edinburgh.

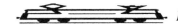
Class '74' Electro-Diesel

An enthusiast has written 'We will miss you' on the front of class '74'
No. 74 010 as it awaits breaking-up on 17 August 1978.
Colin J. Marsden

Railway of origin British Railways
Introduced 1967 (rebuilt from 1959 - introduced class 71)
Manufacturer BR Doncaster
Purpose Mixed traffic, primarily express passenger
Wheel arrangement Bo-Bo
Engine Six-cylinder Paxman 6YJXL diesel producing
650 hp. Locos normally picked up direct from 750 V dc
third rail, giving 2,552 hp
Transmission Electric
Tractive effort 47,500 lb max electric; 40,000 lb max diesel
Number built 10

Developed from the outwardly similar class '71'
Bo-Bo electrics, which could pick up from both
750 V dc third rail and (in certain marshalling yards)
overhead, the ten class '74s' had an on-board diesel
engine to provide power when off the third rail
system – a similar idea to that on the class '73'
electro-diesels. Producing an impressive 2,552 hp
when on straight electric power, the class '74s' were
at home on the few remaining Southampton boat-
train duties in the late 1960s. They could also work
together with electric multiple unit trains, class '33s'
and other electro-diesels. Their lifespan was short,
however, and by the end of 1977 all had been
officially withdrawn from service.

'Kestrel' Prototype

*'Kestrel' leaves Princes Risborough for London Marylebone during its
press run launch of 29 January 1968.*
Euslin Bruce

Railway of origin Private venture on British Railways
Introduced 1967
Manufacturer Hawker Siddeley/Brush Traction,
Loughborough
Purpose Experimental
Wheel arrangement Co-Co
Engine Sixteen-cylinder Sulzer LVA24, giving 4,000 hp
Transmission Electric
Tractive effort Unspecified
Number built 1

During the 1960s, a number of experimental
locomotives underwent proving trials on British
Railways. One of them was No. HS4000 'Kestrel', a
private venture prototype diesel electric designed by
Hawker Siddeley and built by Brush Traction,
Loughborough. Using Sulzer's 4,000 hp 16LVA24
engine, it was designed to operate continuously at
up to 110 mph. Incorporating a number of advanced
features (some of which were eventually taken up in
other BR designs), it was officially handed over to
BR for evaluation on 29 January 1968. Although it
hauled a mammoth 2,028 ton load and ran almost
137,000 miles in the UK, BR did not follow through
with firm orders, and it ended up in the Soviet Union.

Class '50'

During its sunset days, No. 50 003 'Thunderer' was immaculately restored to its original blue livery, and is seen at Laira Depot, Plymouth, during the spring of 1991.
Colin J. Marsden

Railway of origin British Railways
Introduced 1967
Manufacturer English Electric Co, Vulcan Foundry, Newton-le-Willows
Purpose Express passenger
Wheel arrangement Co-Co
Engine Sixteen-cylinder English Electric 16CSVT diesel producing 2,700 hp
Transmission Electric
Tractive effort 48,500 lb max
Number built 50

Originally leased to British Railways by English Electric to provide suitable power north of Crewe on the West Coast Main Line from London Euston to Glasgow, the class '50s' were often seen running in multiple as they headed heavy trains up the famous Shap and Beattock gradients. When electrification finally reached Glasgow, they were put on other duties, but eventually all went to the Western Region where they were named after warships. Mass withdrawals took place in 1990 but the handful still at work in 1991 became celebrity locomotives with enthusiasts, who nicknamed the class 'Hoovers'. Several class '50s' are already in preservation.

Class '87'

*In its original blue livery and before being named, No. 87 001, later
'Royal Scot', stands at Crewe shortly after completion.*
Colin J. Marsden

Railway of origin British Railways
Introduced 1973
Manufacturer British Rail Engineering Ltd, Crewe
Purpose Express passenger
Wheel arrangement Bo-Bo
Traction details 25 kV ac from overhead wires,
transmitted through four GEC traction motors, producing
5,000 hp
Tractive effort 58,000 lb max
Number built 36

The class '87' 25 kV ac electric locomotives were the
last of the 'flat-fronted' designs to be built for the
London Euston–Glasgow West Coast Main Line,
and were brought in to power many of the most
important express trains after the full electrification
into Scotland. Today they share major duties with
the more recently introduced class '90s', and it is
not unusual to see them on freight duties as well.
Built at Crewe between 1973 and 1975, all
eventually acquired names, and one of them,
sub-classified 87/1 and named 'Stephenson', was
built to a more advanced specification. When a class
'87' locomotive is approaching, it can be
distinguished from a class '86' as it has two cab front
windows rather than three.

Class '56'

The class '56' pioneer is No. 56 001 'Whatley'.
Chris Milner

Railway of origin British Railways
Introduced 1976
Manufacturer Electroputere, Craiova, Romania (under contract to Brush Traction), BREL Doncaster and Crewe
Purpose Heavy freight
Wheel arrangement Co-Co
Engine Sixteen-cylinder Ruston Paxman 16RK3CT producing 3,250 hp
Transmission Electric
Tractive effort 61,800 lb max
Number built 135

A familiar sight as they labour along between pit and power station with 'merry-go-round' trains of 1,000 tonnes or more, the class '56' locomotives were designed specifically for these and other taxing heavy freight duties such as the transport of iron ore. Because construction capacity was limited in Britain at the time, the first thirty were built in Romania. After construction switched to BREL at Doncaster – the area around which class '56s' are the most common today – building of the final batch was completed at BREL Crewe in 1984. The class '56s' have slow speed control for the emptying of their hopper wagons at power stations, and their refilling from pitheads, on the move. Under test, a pair of these locomotives shifted more than 3,000 tonnes. They are popular on enthusiasts' passenger trains.

Intercity 125

An Intercity 125 train streaks out of a tunnel mouth.
Chris Milner

Railway of origin British Railways
Introduced 1976
Manufacturer British Rail Engineering Ltd, Crewe
Purpose High-speed passenger
Wheel arrangement Bo-Bo (each of two power cars)
Engine Paxman Valenta twelve-cylinder 12RP200L
producing 2,250 hp in each power car
Transmission Electric
Tractive effort 17,980 lb max each power car
Number built 190-plus power cars

Intercity rail travel in Britain was revolutionised in
1976 with the introduction of the Intercity 125, or
High Speed Train, programme. First utilised on
services out of London Paddington and then on
major services out of London King's Cross,
replacing the 'Deltic' diesel electrics, they brought
new levels of riding quality and speed, with a
maximum designed pace of 125 mph. Their timings
became the fastest in history in Britain, and they
broke many diesel speed records. Later, HSTs
started operating the main passenger services to the
Midlands from London St Pancras and now, with
electrification of the King's Cross-Edinburgh line
complete, they are being cascaded on to cross-
country services, ruling out many requirements for
passengers to change trains *en route*. Each HST has a
power car front and rear.

Class '58'

Class '58' No. 58 050 'Toton Traction Depot' makes a fine sight as it stands on display at Ripple Lane Depot in October 1987.
Colin J. Marsden

Railway of origin British Railways
Introduced 1983
Manufacturer BREL, Doncaster
Purpose Heavy freight
Wheel arrangement Co-Co
Engine Ruston Paxman twelve-cylinder RK3ACT diesel producing 3,300 hp
Transmission Electric
Tractive effort 61,800 lb
Number built 50

Using cheaper construction methods than those which had been applied to the class '56' heavy freight diesel electrics, the class '58' Co-Cos built at British Rail Engineering Ltd, Doncaster, between 1983 and 1987 were intended to give long, reliable and arduous service, principally on the 'merry-go-round' coal trains to power stations. With twelve-cylinder engines instead of the sixteen-cylinder ones used on the class '56', they were specially built to allow any major component to be hoisted off the main frame and replaced quickly, resulting in better availability and lower works bills. They feature simple bonneted engine covers rather than an overall body, and cab access is gained from the rear. The latest Railfreight coal sector livery suits the class well.

Class '59' and '59/1'

No. 59 003 'Yeoman Highlander' stands proudly at Foster-Yeoman's Merehead Quarry.
Colin J. Marsden

Railway of origin British Railways
Introduced 1985
Manufacturer General Motors, La Grange, Illinois, USA
Purpose Heavy freight
Wheel arrangement Co-Co
Engine Sixteen-cylinder 645E3C turbocharged two-stroke diesel producing 3,300 hp
Transmission Electric
Tractive effort 113,550 lb max
Number built Five class '59' and four class '59/1'

The class '59' and later '59/1' Co-Co two-stroke diesel electrics broke new ground by becoming the first American-built diesel locomotives to operate on British Railways. Owned by the aggregates firm of Foster-Yeoman Ltd, and finished in that firm's distinctive blue, white and silver livery, Nos. 59 001-4 became the first to break the mould, being built in 1985 and named 'Yeoman Endeavour', 'Yeoman Enterprise', 'Yeoman Highlander' and 'Yeoman Challenger' in that order. The firm was so pleased by their performance, hauling record loads effortlessly, that it ordered a fifth, No. 59 005, which was named 'Kenneth J. Painter'. In 1990 Associated Roadstone Company (ARC) ordered four of the locomotives from General Motors, and these became classified '59/1' and numbered 59 101-4. These carry names of villages in their operating area.

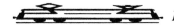
Class '89'

Prior to receiving its name 'Avocet', No. 89 001 stands at Derby in 1988 before setting off for an exhibition in Hamburg.
Colin J. Marsden

Railway of origin British Railways
Introduced 1986
Manufacturer BREL Crewe, sub-contracting for Brush Traction, Loughborough
Purpose Express passenger
Wheel arrangement Co-Co
Power equipment 25 kV ac from overhead equipment, transmission through six Brush TM2201A traction motors, giving 5,850 hp
Tractive effort 46,100 lb
Number built 1

With its cab ends closely following the lines of the experimental Advanced Passenger Train, the unique class '89' Co-Co 25kV ac electric locomotive No. 89 001, later named 'Avocet', was built to a Brush Traction specification at British Rail Engineering Ltd, Crewe, in 1986, and was one of the first electric locomotives to work on the East Coast Main Line as electrification advanced northwards. It headed King's Cross to Peterborough, then Grantham, commuter trains for some months before returning to Brush for modifications. Even though 'Avocet' had many advanced features, not to mention a top speed of 125 mph and fine riding qualities, as a 'non-standard design' its future still appeared uncertain as this book was being completed.

Class '90'

In Railfreight colours, No. 90 043 prepares to leave Manchester Piccadilly Station with a Birmingham train.
Chris Milner

Railway of origin British Railways
Introduced 1987
Manufacturer British Rail Engineering Ltd, Crewe
Purpose Express passenger
Wheel arrangement Bo-Bo
Traction details 25 kV ac from overhead wires, transmitted through four GEC traction motors, producing 5,000 hp
Tractive effort 43,150 lb max
Number built 50

Now a common sight on the London Euston–Glasgow West Coast Main Line, the wedge-fronted class '90' 25 kV ac electric locomotives are in charge of many of the top expresses, often operating in conjunction with a similar-looking driving trailer vehicle at the other end of the train. From these DVTs, as they are called, the driver can operate the locomotive as it 'pushes' at the back of the train, thus ruling out the necessity at terminal stations of bringing out a shunter to detach carriages from a locomotive which is standing at the buffer-stops so that it can 'run round' to the other end of the train. Built at Crewe between 1987 and 1990, the class '90s' have a top operating speed of 110 mph, and have many modern features. Some are owned by the Railfreight sector, and several are named.

Class '91'

No. 91 028 streaks through Huntingdon in 1991.
Chris Milner

Railway of origin British Railways
Introduced 1988
Manufacturer BREL Crewe Works/GEC-Alsthom
Purpose High-speed express passenger
Wheel arrangement Bo-Bo
Power equipment 25 kV ac from overhead equipment.
Transmission through four GEC G426AZ traction motors,
giving 6,300 hp
Tractive effort Still being assessed
Number built 30

The most powerful electric locomotives in Britain,
designed for a top speed of 140 mph, the sleek class
'91s' are the flagships of the newly electrified East
Coast Main Line from London King's Cross to
Edinburgh. On 26 September 1991 one of them,
No. 91 012, broke the rail record between the two
capitals, completing the journey with five of the new
Mk IV carriages and a driving van trailer in tow in
3 hr 29 min exactly – an average speed of 112.9 mph.
Speeds of 140 mph were reached several times *en
route*. Although in service these locomotives are
restricted to 125 mph until signalling improvements
are carried out, their vast reserves of power make
them capable of making up time in a way that has
never been possible in Britain before. Class '91'
locomotives are also unusual in that they have one
streamlined cab end and one completely flat cab end.

Class '60'

No. 60 002 'Capability Brown' stands at Derby in October 1989.
Colin J. Marsden

Railway of origin British Railways
Introduced 1989
Manufacturer Brush Traction, Loughborough
Purpose Heavy freight
Wheel arrangement Co-Co
Engine Mirrlees Eight-cylinder MB275T diesel producing 3,100 hp
Transmission Electric
Tractive effort 100,000 lb plus
Number built 100

The latest and most stylish freight-only locomotives to be built for British Railways, the class '60' Co-Co diesel-electrics embody a host of features enabling them to haul extremely heavy freight trains single-handed, thus making many older and less powerful diesel electric locomotives redundant. Unusually for any class these days, the '60s' have all been bestowed with names from the start, featuring subjects such as mountains and important characters from Britain's industrial history. At the heart of the locomotive is an eight-cylinder Mirrlees MB275T diesel churning out 3,100 hp at 1,000 rpm, driving the wheels through six separately excited traction motors. They can put down a staggering 100,000 lb plus at maximum tractive effort. In their smart grey Railfreight colour scheme, they are set to become a familiar sight in many areas of Britain.

Class '150' 'Sprinter' Unit

Class '150' 'Sprinter' unit No. 150 147 at Salford Crescent, Manchester.
Gavin W. Morrison

Railway of origin British Railways
Introduced 1984
Manufacturer British Rail Engineering Ltd, York
Purpose Medium-distance passenger
Formation Two or three-car units
Engine Cummins NT855R5 diesel, producing 285 hp
Number built 120-plus

When, in the 1980s, it became obvious that British
Rail's 'first-generation' diesel multiple unit fleet
dating from the late 1950s (which itself replaced
many hundreds of steam locomotives and their
carriages) was becoming life-expired, a massive
effort was launched to find effective replacement
trains, and the class '150' 'Sprinters' were among
the results. Built at the York Works of BREL, they
are now at work in many parts of the country, some
in regional transport authority liveries. A number of
them were refurbished at Eastleigh, near
Southampton, as West Midlands 'Centro' trains, and
among their duties in this guise have been long
forays along the attractive Cambrian Line from
Birmingham to Aberystwyth and Pwllheli.

Class '142' 'Pacer' Unit

Class '142' 'Pacer' unit No. 142 009, in Greater Manchester PTE
orange and brown colours, at Millhouses, Sheffield.
Gavin W. Morrison

Railway of origin British Railways
Introduced 1985
Manufacturer Leyland/BREL
Purpose Branch line and local commuter services
Formation Two-car
Engine Leyland TL11 diesel producing 205 hp
Number built 96 plus variants

With each vehicle unusually based on a simple four-wheel chassis, the two-car 'Pacer' units were built for utmost economy, and can be seen in several parts of Britain in the colour schemes of various local transport authorities as well as BR's own Regional Railways livery. They are ideally suited to shorter journeys in major urban areas, with frequent stops, but also venture into the countryside on longer trips, such as along the Esk Valley line from Middlesbrough to Whitby. The 'Pacers' have probably been the key to keeping open a number of passenger routes which might otherwise have been forced to close through economic considerations. A re-engining plan using Cummins power units was announced recently.

Class '158' 'Express' Unit

Two class '158' two-car units, led by No. 158 725, leave Forres, on the Aberdeen–Inverness line.
Gavin W. Morrison

Railway of origin British Railways
Introduced 1989
Manufacturer BREL, Derby Litchurch Lane
Purpose Main line and cross-country express passenger
Formation Two or three cars
Engine Cummins NTA855R diesel producing 350 hp
Number built 170-plus

Regional Railways' fast and stylish air-conditioned 'Express' diesel unit trains have brought new levels of comfort, sophistication and speed to a large number of major routes such as Norwich–Birmingham, Liverpool–Newcastle, and Manchester–Cardiff, and taking over from locomotive-hauled trains on the important Glasgow Queen Street–Edinburgh Waverley corridor. A Network SouthEast version designated class '159' has also been chosen to take over on the Waterloo–Exeter route. With their well-proven capacity for long-distance travel in true main line comfort, the class '158s' have an assured future now that some annoying teething troubles have been sorted out.

Class '153' Single-Car Unit

Class '153' single-car unit No. 153 376 at Sleaford, Lincs, during a press demonstration run during the spring of 1992.
Peter Kelly

Railway of origin British Railways
Introduced 1991, as single-car rebuilds of class '155' multiple units (introduced 1988) with two driving ends
Manufacturer Leyland Bus; conversions at Hunslet-Barclay, Kilmarnock
Purpose Light rural branch line services
Formation Single-car, from former two-car sets
Engine Cummins NT855R5 diesel, producing 285 hp
Number built 42 two-car sets originally

Built originally as two-car class '155' units, these Leyland-bodied vehicles, becoming known as the 'Rural Railbus' or 'Bubble Cars', are being reconstructed as single-car diesel units and designated class '153'. They can be operated economically to replace worn-out 'first generation' diesel multiple units on quieter lines in rural areas such as Lincolnshire and Gloucestershire. Their construction shows a laudable commitment by Regional Railways to continue services on lines which might once have been under threat of closure to passenger traffic.

LOCOMOTIVES INCLUDED IN THIS BOOK

Type	Wheels	Railway of Origin	Designer	Year	Page
STEAM					
4F	0-6-0	MR/LMSR	Sir H. Fowler	1911/24	18
5700	0-6-0PT	GWR	C. B. Collett	1929	40
A1	4-6-2	LNER	E. Thompson/A. H. Peppercorn	1945/48	68
A3	4-6-2	LNER	Sir H. N. Gresley	1927	35
A4	4-6-2	LNER	Sir H. N. Gresley	1935	50
Adams Radial	4-4-2T	LSWR	W. Adams	1882	11
B1	4-6-0	LNER	E. Thompson	1942	63
'Battle of Britain'	4-6-2	SR	O. V. S. Bulleid	1946	70
Beyer-Garratt	2-8-8-2T	LNER	Beyer Peacock/Sir H. N. Gresley	1925	30
Beyer-Garratt	2-6-6-2T	LMSR	Beyer Peacock/Sir H. Fowler	1927	38
'Big Bertha'	0-10-0	MR	Sir H. Fowler	1919	23
'Black Five'	4-6-0	LMSR	Sir W. H. Stanier	1934	47
'Britannia'	4-6-2	BR	BR Derby/Crewe	1951	77
'Castle'	4-6-0	GWR	C. B. Collett	1923	26
'City'	4-4-0	GWR	G. J. Churchward	1903	17

Type	Wheels	Railway of Origin	Designer	Year	Page
'Clan'	4-6-2	BR	BR Derby/Crewe	1952	78
Class 27 goods	0-6-0	LYR	J. A. F. Aspinall	1889	15
'Coronation'	4-6-2	LMSR	Sir W. A. Stanier	1937	54
'County'	4-6-0	GWR	F. W. Hawksworth	1945	66
'Crab'	2-6-0	LMSR	G. Hughes	1926	34
'Dukedog'	4-4-0	GWR	C. B. Collett	1936	52
G2	0-8-0	LNWR	C. J. Bowen-Cooke	1921	25
'Grange'	4-6-0	GWR	C. B. Collett	1936	51
'Hall'	4-6-0	GWR	C. B. Collett	1924/28	27
Ivatt class 2	2-6-0	LMSR	H. G. Ivatt	1946	71
Ivatt class 2	2-6-2T	LMSR	H. G. Ivatt	1946	67
Ivatt class 4	2-6-0	LMSR	H. G. Ivatt	1947	72
J15	0-6-0	GER	T. W. Worsdell/H. Holden	1883	12
J36	0-6-0	NBR	M. Holmes	1888	14
'Jinty'	0-6-0T	LMSR	Sir H. Fowler	1924	28
'Jubilee'	4-6-0	LMSR	Sir W. A. Stanier	1934	48
K4	2-6-0	LNER	Sir H. N. Gresley	1937	56
'King'	4-6-0	GWR	C. B. Collett	1927	36

LOCOMOTIVES INCLUDED IN THIS BOOK

Type	Wheels	Railway of Origin	Designer	Year	Page
'King Arthur'	4-6-0	LSWR	R. W. Urie	1918	22
'Large Director'	4-4-0	GCR	J. G. Robinson	1920	24
'Large Prairie'	2-6-2T	GWR	C. B. Collett	1928	39
'Lord Nelson'	4-6-0	SR	R. E. L. Maunsell	1926	33
'Manor'	4-6-0	GWR	C. B. Collett	1938	57
'Merchant Navy'	4-6-2	SR	O. V. S. Bulleid	1941	59
Midland 'Spinner'	4-2-2	MR	S. W. Johnson	1887	13
N2	0-6-2T	LNER	Sir H. N. Gresley	1925	31
N7	0-6-2T	GER/LNER	A. J. Hill	1915/25	32
P1	2-8-2	LNER	Sir H. N. Gresley	1925	29
'Patriot'	4-6-0	LMSR	Sir M. Fowler	1930/33	42
'Princess Royal'	4-6-2	LMSR	Sir W. A. Stanier	1933	45
Q1	0-6-0	SR	O. V. S. Bulleid	1942	62
'Queen' (I)	4-6-0	GSR(I)	E. C. Bredin	1939	58
Robinson 2-8-0	2-8-0	GCR	J. G. Robinson	1911	19
'Royal Scot'	4-6-0	LMSR	Sir H. Fowler/Sir W. A. Stanier	1927/43	64
S15	4-6-0	SR	R. E. L. Maunsell	1927	37

Type	Wheels	Railway of Origin	Designer	Year	Page
S&D 2-8-0	2-8-0	SDJR	Sir H. Fowler	1914	20
'Schools'	4-4-0	SR	R. E. L. Maunsell	1930	43
Standard class 2	2-6-0	BR	Des. BR Derby	1953	84
Standard Class 4	2-6-0	BR	Des. BR Doncaster	1953	83
Standard class 4	4-6-0	BR	Des. BR Brighton	1951	80
Standard class 4	2-6-4T	BR	Des. BR Brighton	1951	81
Standard class 5	4-6-0	BR	Des. BR Doncaster	1951	79
Standard class 8P	4-6-2	BR	Des. BR Derby	1954	86
Standard class 9F	2-10-0	BR	Des. BR Brighton	1954	87
Stanier 8F	2-8-0	LMSR	Sir W. A. Stanier	1935	49
Stanier Mogul	2-6-0	LMSR	Sir W. A. Stanier	1933	46
Stirling 'Single'	4-2-2	GNR	P. Stirling	1870	9
T9	4-4-0	LSWR	D. Drummond	1899	16
'Terrier'	0-6-0T	LBSCR	W. Stroudley	1872	10
U(I)	4-4-0	GNR(I)	G. T. Glover	1915	21
U	2-6-0	SR	R. E. L. Maunsell	1928	41
USA	0-6-0T	USATC/SR	Vulcan Wks, USA	1942	61
V2	2-6-2	LNER	Sir H. N. Gresley	1936	53

LOCOMOTIVES INCLUDED IN THIS BOOK

Type	Wheels	Railway of Origin	Designer	Year	Page
V(I)	4-4-0	GNR(I)	G. T. Glover	1932	44
WI	4-6-4	LNER	Sir H. N. Gresley	1937	55
WD 2-10-0	2-10-0	WD	R. A. Riddles	1943	65
'West Country'	4-6-2	SR	O. V. S. Bulleid	1945	69
DIESEL					
'Baby Deltic'	Bo-Bo	BR	English Electric	1959	97
'Blue Pullman'	n/a	BR	Metropolitan-Cammell	1959	99
Class 08	0-6-0	BR	BR various	1953	85
Class 17	Bo-Bo	BR	Clayton/Beyer Peacock	1962	108
Class 20	Bo-Bo	BR	English Electric	1957	89
Class 24	Bo-Bo	BR	BR various	1958	91
Class 26	Bo-Bo	BR	BRCW	1958	92
Class 31	A1A-A1A	BR	Brush Traction	1957	90
Class 33	Bo-Bo	BR	BRCW	1959	98
Class 37	Co-Co	BR	English Electric/RSH	1960	100
Class 40	1 Co-Co 1	BR	English Electric/RSH	1958	95

Type	Wheels	Railway of Origin	Designer	Year	Page
Class 46	1 Co-Co 1	BR	BR	1961	103
Class 47	Co-Co	BR	Brush Traction/BR	1962	107
Class 50	Co-Co	BR	English Electric	1967	115
Class 55 'Deltic'	Co-Co	BR	English Electric	1961	102
Class 56	Co-Co	BR	Electroputere, Romania/BREL Doncaster	1976	117
Class 58	Co-Co	BR	BREL Doncaster	1983	119
Class 59, 59/1	Co-Co	Foster Yeoman/ARC/BR	General Motors, Illinois, USA	1985	120
Class 60	Co-Co	BR	Brush Traction	1989	124
DP2	Co-Co	BR	English Electric	1962	110
'Deltic' prototype		Private venture on BR	English Electric	1955	88
Fell diesel-mechanical	4-8-4	BR	H. G. Ivatt/Lt-Col L. F. R. Fell	1951	75
'Hymek'	B-B	BR	Beyer Peacock	1961	105
InterCity 125	n/a	BR	BREL Crewe	1976	118

LOCOMOTIVES INCLUDED IN THIS BOOK

Type	Wheels	Railway of Origin	Designer	Year	Page
'Kestrel'	Co-Co	Private venture on BR	Hawker Siddeley/Brush Traction	1967	114
'Lion'	Co-Co	Private venture on BR			
Metrovick Type 2	Co-Bo	BR	BRCW	1962	111
Nos. 10000/1	Co-Co	BR	BR/Metropolitan Vickers	1958	96
Nos. 10201-3	1 Co-Co 1	LMSR	Derby Works	1947	73
'Warship'	A1A-A1A	BR	Ashford Works	1951	76
'Warship'	B-B	BR	North British	1958	93
'Western'	C-C	BR	BR Swindon	1958	94
		BR	BR Swindon/Crewe	1961	104
DIESEL MULTIPLE UNITS/RAILCARS					
'Bubble' class 153	n/a	BR	Leyland Bus/Hunslet Barclay	1991	128
'Express' class 158	n/a	BR	BREL Derby	1989	127

Type	Wheels	Railway of Origin	Designer	Year	Page
'Pacer' class 142	n/a	BR	Leyland/BREL	1985	126
'Sprinter' class 150	n/a	BR	BREL York	1984	125
GAS-TURBINE					
GT3	4-6-0	Private venture on BR			101
No. 18000	A1A-A1A	BR	English Electric	1961	101
No. 18100	Co-Co	BR	Swiss Locomotive & Machine Works	1950	74
		BR	Metropolitan Vickers	1952	82
ELECTRO-DIESEL					
Class 73	Bo-Bo	BR	BR Eastleigh/English Electric	1962	109
Class 74	Bo-Bo	BR	BR Doncaster	1967	113
ELECTRIC					
Class 85	Bo-Bo	BR	BR Doncaster	1961	106
Class 86	Bo-Bo	BR	English Electric/BR Doncaster	1965	112
Class 87	Bo-Bo	BR	BREL Crewe	1973	116

LOCOMOTIVES INCLUDED IN THIS BOOK

Type	Wheels	Railway of Origin	Designer	Year	Page
Class 89	Co-Co	BR	Brush Traction/BREL Crewe	1986	121
Class 90	Bo-Bo	BR	BREL Crewe	1987	122
Class 91	Bo-Bo	BR	GEC Alsthom/BREL Crewe	1988	123
Nos. 20001-3	Co-Co	SR	Ashford Works	1941/8	60

Abbreviations:

BR	British Railways
GCR	Great Central Railway
GER	Great Eastern Railway
GNR	Great Northern Railway
GNR(I)	Great Northern Railway (Ireland)
GSR(I)	Great Southern Railway (Ireland)
GWR	Great Western Railway
LBSCR	London, Brighton & South Coast Railway
LMSR	London, Midland & Scottish Railway
LNER	London & North Eastern Railway
LNWR	London & North Western Railway
LSWR	London & South Western Railway
LYR	Lancashire & Yorkshire Railway
MR	Midland Railway
NBR	North British Railway
SDJR	Somerset & Dorset Joint Railway
SR	Southern Railway
USATC	United States Army Transportation Corps
WD	War Department